AMERICAN SOCIETY

AMERICAN SOCIETY

INTERPRETATIONS OF EDUCATIONAL AND OTHER FORCES

BY
CHARLES FRANKLIN THWING

Essay Index Reprint Series

BOOKS FOR LIBRARIES PRESS
FREEPORT, NEW YORK

First Published 1931
Reprinted 1970

STANDARD BOOK NUMBER:
8369-1729-4

LIBRARY OF CONGRESS CATALOG CARD NUMBER:
75-117856

PRINTED IN THE UNITED STATES OF AMERICA

FROM
THE HIBBERT JOURNAL
1911-1930

PREFACE

Does not Aristotle say that in any investigation the first step is to ask a question? In this case, the second step is to find an answer. Yet both question and answer lead to interpretations. It is to interpretations that this little book is devoted. It is an attempt to interpret American life in a few of its manifold elements and characteristics.

The book is, however, composed of interpretations limited in time as well as in its field of study. The time is the score of years pregnant between 1911 and 1930. The period covers the years of the Great War as well as the years immediately preceding and the decade following its close. Beginning with a general consideration of the best and worst in America, it seeks to interpret that fundamental institution known as the family. This interpretation is followed by the presentation of the motives which led the Pilgrims to come to America, and to an evaluation of the contribution which they made to the colonial and other commonwealths. In the fourth chapter it presents some evidences of the effect of the war on the higher learning. There follows a comparison between the European War and the Civil War in America. This comparison is succeeded by chapters on the prospect of liberal learning after the war, on public opinion in the United States in the dark years of the war, and by a specific study of American society following the signing of the treaty of peace. To the war chapters there succeeds a consideration of the ideas and principles which rule in America. This chapter is followed by a weighing of the tests which constitute civilization, and in particular it seeks to answer the question whether American civilization can meet these tests. The book concludes with a consideration of the growth and development of institutions in the United States.

There are two common atmospheres which seem to possess and to unite these chapters. The first relates to the intellectual liberty and independence of the individual. It is a liberty to think one's thoughts, to form one's philosophy, to make one's choices, to do one's work, to suffer one's failures, and to exult in one's triumphs. But to the liberty of the individual is to be added the liberty of the commonwealth both organized and unorganized,—the liberty of opportunities and privileges, the liberty of statute and of common law. The second and allied atmosphere which moves through these pages represents the essential elements of the worth of education. For in education are found a liberalizing mind, a sense of idealism, a power to realize ideals, a proportional understanding of human values, an altruistic sympathy with all men, and an appreciation of the divine in humanity.

Out of these diverse and yet united interpretations, and of a common atmosphere of liberty and of the value of education, is born a hope high, a belief broad, and an understanding deep of the future of America and of the triumph of its institutions. The hope, the belief, and the understanding, be it also said, are not limited to America, but do represent and intimate the ultimate triumph of the best in the whole world.

C. F. T.

Western Reserve University,
Cleveland, Ohio,
4th July, 1930.

librarian was:

in attending a more advanced,
  skills session? Yes ___ No___

 ents on the library skills
 ing you had not known but learned

F1788.D69

F1788.W9

D16.8.Z48

CONTENTS

	PAGE
PREFACE	v
I. THE BEST AND THE WORST IN AMERICAN SOCIETY	1
II. THE AMERICAN FAMILY	40
III. THE PILGRIMS' MOTIVE AND CONTRIBUTION	58
IV. THE EFFECT OF THE EUROPEAN WAR ON HIGHER LEARNING IN AMERICAN SOCIETY	70
V. THE AMERICAN CIVIL WAR AND THE GREAT WAR: A COMPARISON	92
VI. PROSPECTS OF LIBERAL EDUCATION AFTER THE GREAT WAR	121
VII. PUBLIC OPINION IN THE UNITED STATES IN THE LAST THREE YEARS: 1914-1917	144
VIII. AMERICAN SOCIETY AFTER THE GREAT WAR	169
IX. RULING IDEAS IN AMERICAN SOCIETY	187
X. WHAT ARE THE TESTS OF A NATION'S CIVILIZATION? CAN AMERICA MEET THEM?	221
XI. GROWTH OF INSTITUTIONS IN AMERICAN SOCIETY	243
INDEX	265

AMERICAN SOCIETY

AMERICAN SOCIETY

I

THE BEST AND THE WORST IN AMERICAN SOCIETY[*]

A FEW months ago an Englishman, of distinguished name and rich achieving, wrote me, saying: "My *God,* what a country is yours! But what the *devil* is it all coming to? . . . My mind, when I was in America in the spring, oscillated between two extremes. At one moment I would be saying 'This is the nearest thing to heaven yet achieved.' At the next I would cry out 'Hell is an accomplished fact!' " These vigorous phrases are, however, only the emotional expressions of the deep quickenings of a reverent character and understanding mind, kindled by diverse experiences and contrasted observations. Such interpretations are not to be accepted lightly or wantonly, but reverently, soberly, discreetly, advisedly. I shall, therefore, seek to deal with them in a spirit of the utmost seriousness. For they relate to things fundamental.

As a result of pondering over these pious profanities, and seeking to classify them, I have been asking, What is the best and what is the worst in

[*] July, 1926.

America? To this question I want to make answer. In fact I wish to give no less than six answers.

The best in American as in any society is found in the individual person. The doctrine of Calvin is believed and practiced in American society. He the individual, in Geneva or elsewhere, is the crown of the whole evolutionary process. He, standing single and alone, is the best and is the most impressive figure in the New as he is in the Old World. Yet some would declare that the individual creates and finds his best self, not in himself alone, but in himself as a member of a group. The opposite of the statement is quite as true. The worst in American life is indeed the individual. But also this worst takes on possibly a worse worst when he surrounds himself by his fellow devils. The worst personality is created and is found, as is the case with the best, in the group. The devil in each of us becomes the more devilish by reason of hellish companionship. One cannot fail to recall some of Dante's cantos.

Yet returns the more definite question, in and for the individual himself, what is the best and what is the worst?

In the typical individual of the United States the best lies in his use of personal liberty. He, this American, is given a degree of personal liberty more free than is found in most communities. The Declaration of Independence of 1776 added to the bounds of that freedom. That instrument gave recognition to rights formerly denied to the individual, or which he held as reluctantly given gifts. Yet, though being an individual, free-born and free-constituted, he does not fail to recognize that there are other individuals quite as free-born and with equal right to free activity. If he be at all thoughtful, he appreciates the truth that a democracy is a rule of all the people. Such a recognition represents two things—first, intelligence, and, secondly, a sense of volitional and emotional altruism. The flaming eloquences of the Declaration of 1776 were in less than half a generation succeeded by the sober statements of the Constitution. It is under the guardianship and instructions of the articles of that Constitution that the American individual lives and moves and has his being. The best in his freedom is wisely and securely protected in and by and for the best for all, and the best for all also assures to himself, under wise and secure guardianship, the best. The constancy of the continuance of this best blinds the ordinary citizen to its priceless worth. But, to the reflective citizen, this consistent beneficence, in act and in atmosphere, has meaning inexpressible.

Yet this best easily passes over into the worst. Bodies terrestrial or celestial, left to themselves, fall. Liberty passes over into tolerance, tolerance gravitates into laxity, laxity moves down into license, license finds an easy passage to lawlessness, lawlessness spells disobedience, disobedience results in disintegration, and disintegration almost necessarily ends in destruction. The individual, in his freedom, is liable to suffer disintegration, and disintegration is a sign-post to nothingness for himself, and to causes or conditions in others inciting to similar suffering or negativeness or annihilation. One teaching to be derived from such personal lapses is that if the individual is to have free access to powder-magazines he should be taught to realize that, under certain conditions, powder-magazines do explode. This is a lesson which not only certain parts of the new republic in America, but also all the new republics of Central and Eastern Europe of the present year and decade, would do well to heed. That a few are heeding is cause of rejoicing.

A second element of the best and of the worst of the individual is found in the contrasted ideas of idealism and sordidness. The typical American is idealistic. He is a child of the imagination: he sees visions; he dreams dreams. The future means more than the present, and the present is not without deep meanings. In his mind is a certain yonderness. "Over there" is quite as significant as "right here." Perhaps the strongest evidence of the idealism of his character is the use of his material treasure in human beneficence. This use is both communal and individualistic, and at times in super-Crœsus amounts. It is said that Mr. John D. Rockefeller has given away more than half a billion dollars. His son, bearing his name, continues in the great progression. Mr. Carnegie gave away about four hundred million dollars. These gifts went largely into foundations, established on human and humane bases, designed to serve causes as broad and diverse as education of many types—collegiate, medical research—as religion, also of many types of the Christian faith. All peoples, too, are beneficiaries of tens of thousands of individual gifts both large and small. If the names of Carnegie and Rockefeller are most outstanding, other names are also noteworthy. There lies before me as I write a long list of persons who have contributed from small sums up to more than two hundred thousand dollars toward the fifteen-million dollar fund for the erection of the Cathedral of St. John the Divine in New York City. In fact, it is said that New York City alone contributes every year no less than eighty million dollars to charitable and social needs. I estimate that in the great cities there are given every year about a million dollars for each section of a hundred thousand people for charitable and social beneficence. After subtracting all unworthy motives for this beneficence, after eliminating all narrow outlooks into the field of human betterment, there still stand the belief and the conviction that these vast sums are the result of individual vision, imagination, idealism.

By the side of this best, however, lies the worst. The worst bears the names of avarice, covetousness, greed, mammon. With these bad names is to be joined possibly a worse one, namely, the word dishonesty—dishonesty under two laws, the statute and the moral. For there is a greed which is itself bad enough, but there is a greed which leads to a still worse one, which, in getting its purpose, breaks the laws of man, defying courts, and succeeding in putting off the law of God. Examples of such fits of iniquity emerge from time to time in American society and American courts. Not long ago there was litigation in a remote Western State regarding certain lawlessness known as the "Teapot Dome" case. This case, in its slimy trails and dirty traces, touched high officers of the official Government, the chief officers of great corporations, and many citizens of good names. But, before or after testifying, such citizens fled the country—to Mexico or France. "It is all such a mass of pollution," said an attorney for the prosecution to me, "that one is almost ashamed of being a man." And why have these things been done? They, these officers of the State, have done these things under the very motive which Daniel Webster attributed to the murderer of Captain White, of Salem, in the year 1830. "It was," said Mr. Webster, "a cool, calculating, money-making murder."[1] This case is a case of "calculating, money-making" stealing, and stealing carried on under the cloak of a public trust. It is damnable. Alas, it is not unique. It possibly might be called an application of Rousseau's doc-

[1] *Works*, Vol. VI, p. 52.

trine that, in any offending, the individual is innocent and society guilty.

Another chief part of the best and of the worst, touching the individual, lies in the field of his efficiency and of his consequent nerve exhaustion. The American plans largely, magnificently. He executes swiftly and also magnificently. For his undertakings—mining, shipping, railroads, steel mills, distribution of goods—he has, as for his beneficences, far-flung visions and imaginations. In the carrying forward of his undertakings he is a big borrower at the banks. He mobilizes the great forces of labor, union and non-union. He calls into his service associates of a vision and power like unto his own—groups for buying, for selling, for publicity, as well as for making. He spends immense sums in building up an effective organization. That organization may spread throughout the forty-eight individual States. These branches, indeed, may cover the globe, and are likely to be numbered by the thousands. The gossamer threads of commerce, the cables of industrialism, go over and under and through the earth. But they go out, be it remembered, from a single orienting head, or from a single administrative, or executive, group. It is indeed magnificent. It belongs to those fundamental "cosmical phenomena" of which Herbert Spencer once wrote: "Such imaginations as we can frame of those vast cosmical phenomena amid which 'our little lives' are passed—to think, for example, that while the eye has been passing from the beginning of this line to the end of it, the Earth has travelled thirty miles!"[2]

But what of the nether side of such magnificence and munificence? For there is a nether side. It is the side which Herbert Spencer also noticed and commented upon when on his visit to the United States—"American life," he characterized by "over-devotion to work."[3] It is the result created by the excess of the virtue of efficiency. It is called by diverse names. It gravitates downward: from overwork it passes to nerve strain, from nerve strain to nerve exhaustion, from nerve exhaustion to breakdown. It means growing old before one's proper time. It spells hardened arteries, weak heart, premature decay, and, in many cases, early death, or, what is worse, permanent invalidism in both body and mind.

But with such a result created by efficiency is to be connected a not dissimilar result coming from a wholly different cause, a cause or condition of inefficiency. This condition of inefficiency is a movement, or a part of a movement, swift and tumultuous. This movement is, for my present interpretation, personal and individual. It represents a swiftness and tumultuousness as applied even to the zone of recreation or of amusement. This zone stands for rather unique freedom of living allowed to youth. Into the jungle of amuse-

[2] *An Autobiography*, by Herbert Spencer, Vol. II, p. 461.
[3] *Ibid.*, p. 479.

ment youth of both sexes plunge. Ideas are many and superficial, emotions strong, experiences, begun early in life, rapid. Many a young American man or woman has lived more in the first twenty years than has the Englishman or the Frenchman in the first thirty. Many cannot stand the racket. Brain storms abound. Brain exhaustions follow each other by swift turns. Emotional thundershowers break. In the lack of steadying principles the youth goes to pieces. His brain is wrecked, and even his character. Of course, such extreme results are not common. But too frequent are they not to demand a passing remark. Perhaps I especially feel the force of this condition at the present moment. For within three weeks two friends of mine, youths of the emotional type, yet liberally educated, have taken their own lives, the younger immediately before having shot a woman, his companion.

In all the field of the best and the worst, as embodied in the individual, lies the field social, the field of the community, the community informal and unorganized.

In passing to this section, which I call the social, it may be said, almost parenthetically, that Socialism in almost any one of its many definitions, as opposed to individualism, has so far failed to get any popular following in the United States. The soil is not fitted to this tree of good and of evil. The agitator is given a hearing. A few adherents, occasionally, in consequence of too inflammatory utterances, are put into prison cells. Equality of opportunity works against them, as well as do reputed liberty and democratic fraternity. A country in which one-half the people either own land or have a deposit in the savings bank does not make an atmosphere for the left wing, or perhaps for any wing, of Socialism to fly in.

In this general social field, as a central unit, belongs the family. The family, ranking with the civil Government, the Church, the school, literature, and property, is a chief, or some would add the chief, institution of society. The monogamous family is still regnant. The splendid outcome of an historic struggle of unknown length, reënforced by the teaching of Christ, supported by the Catholic and the Protestant Church, it remains as the most historic, and as still the most formative, of all social and civil institutions. But by its side, or as a serpent lodged in its bosom and poisoning its life, lies the principle, or method, of excessive individualism. Individualism is indeed always excessive. For it is too great or too intense individuality. But individualism, as opposed to the family, calls out special emphasis. For the family represents a uniting, and in the uniting a harmonizing and adjustment of of two individualities. In the United States these individualities seem to be menaced by the peculiar peril of legal separation. Of course, legal separation results ultimately from personal separateness. This peril, advanced to its extreme limit, comes to be known by the technical name of divorce. In America divorces, like murder, are many times more common than in the Mother Country. In many counties of several States one marriage in every ten results in divorce. The legal causes are many, running from adultery to incompatibility or prolonged absence. They include both collisions and collusions. Of course, the overhead and underlying cause, as I have intimated, is excessive individualism, a quality, or plant, of human nature which seems to have especially rank growth in American soil. With this cause is to be united the condition of the enlarging opportunities open to women for independent careers, careers which are now listed as numbering no less than one hundred and eighty-three—a good, of course, in itself, but accompanied with perils. The present breakdown of the American family is one of the worst of all evils, as its integrity is one of the best elements of the whole American social system. A hopeful sign, however, is the recognition of the evil.

In the enlargement of opportunities for careers for women one good element, however, should not be passed over. It represents the transit of the English movement of training daughters of the family in and for self-support. The French movement of assuming that all daughters will marry has its disadvantages. The English method of assuming and educating them for whatever may await, marriage or no marriage, has far greater advantages. The American home adopts the method of the home of the Mother Country.

This breakdown of the family, it may be added, is one of the chief causes of the prevalence of crimes, crimes committed by boys—by boys of the age of, or under the age of, eighteen. The number of murders committed by such youths seems to be exceeded only by the number of manslaughterings committed by drivers of automobiles. For the moral standards set by mothers and fathers in the home are either lacking or, if not lacking, are distressingly low and loose. But when the home is actually destroyed, or when it is on the critical line of being destroyed, the children lose what should be the most constructive force of and for moral strengthening and moral direction.

A second social condition relates to the respect, or to the lack of respect, paid to the Federal Constitution (this is also political, of which more presently)—the lack of respect paid to laws, and the excessiveness of the sympathy given to those who have been accused, or convicted, of breaking the laws. The Federal Constitution, however, does seem to maintain its integrity and majesty. It is amended from time to time, although only nineteen amendments have been passed since its adoption in 1789. But the difficulty of amending, requiring the vote of thirty-two of the forty-eight States, intimates the popular judgment regarding its sacredness. It is, in a sense, still in the making, but it is not in a making so active and immediate as belongs to the like, and the unlike, unwritten English instrument. The Supreme Court, a body which, to a degree, may be said to administer, or at least to interpret, the Constitution, remains the most respected, and probably the most important, of all the institutions of the Republic. The impairment of this respect would be a dire peril.

Underneath this happy condition are found numberless and diverse statutes passed by the Federal Congress—fifty thousand have been passed since its first session—and by the legislatures of the forty-eight States. These statutes are, as is well known, rather broken than kept. Punishments for breaking are also notoriously lax and unworthy of the seriousness of the offending. Punishments for homicide, in the various grades of guiltiness, are peculiarly lax. Many murderers never come to trial. More are let off with what seem to the layman to be peculiarly light sentences, and more yet, or at least many, are paroled after a brief term of good behavior in prison. Few serve out a term, and fewer are executed. But what is possibly yet more significant than these facts is the current sympathy on the part of the community for the condemned murderer. "That wretch, half insane," "Give the poor dog a chance; he never had one," are popular verdicts. Pardon for the accused, guilty or guiltless, is far more common than condemnation of him or indignation for his presumed crime. A maudlin sentiment abounds. The result is that killing is one of the safest of all crimes. If the remark did not seem flippant, I would say that murdering is one of the most interesting of all sports. The condition is one which demands the reading of some of the great lines in Dante's *Inferno*. It seems to be a distressing development of what De Tocqueville said three-quarters of a century ago: "In no country is criminal justice administered with more mildness than in the United States."[4]

In happy contrast with such shameless immoralities and disgusting sympathies bulks large and vigorous the care given to the physical health of the whole community and of its individual members. This care has its beginning in the researches of the medical schools and of the medical institutes, researches which in turn find their special origin in the laboratories of German university professors and of Pasteur. These laboratory researches both inform and quicken the health boards of individual commonwealths, of great cities, and even of small towns. These health boards in turn are alert guardians against occasional epidemics and contagion, and, what is more important, they promote regular inspection of markets or of other food centers. They establish clinics for school children and other social groups. The promotion of the physical health of the American community is one of its most precious assets

[4] *Democracy in America*, by Alexis De Tocqueville, Vol. II., p. 203.

in both fact and method. It is a result of the advance made by the medical profession in the last fifty years, an advance greater than that made by any other profession. Health associations, covering the whole country, have become powerful as well as local societies efficient. The Red Cross is perhaps the most outstanding—a watchman on the wall of our hygienic Zion, a private soldier in the armies of health. The American Medical Association, interpreting and guiding unto sound general conditions, the National Safety Council, the Rockefeller, the Commonwealth, and other Foundations, hospital and nursing associations, serving in many relations, these and numerous other foundations represent new and mighty forces for the promotion of the health of the general community.

But in this field in which good wheat is sown are also sown tares, and both are growing together. There is no country which suffers so many medical quackeries and of a variety so diverse and pestiferous. The race is a large one indeed. Its birth is found in the bogus medical schools which issue bogus diplomas to consequent bogus doctors. It is enlarged by the contributions of the pseudo-religious cults. The field for its growth and for the development of its cultures is found in ignorance and superstition. It makes a special appeal to the moron, or the semi-moron, and to the superficial mind of ignorant, even if sincere, disciples. It is supported by the fears and the cowardice felt in the face of honest and thorough diagnosis.

In the social field of the United States, too, as in the social field of most countries, the worst relates to things (at least in parts) and the best relates to persons. America is constantly declared to be materialistic. The remark, which is usually made as an indictment, is true. It is concerned with physical aspects and emphases. It cannot and should not be, in a new country of vast resources, otherwise. The appeal made to the senses is dominant, and the responsiveness of the senses is domineering. But the appeal is not so dominant, nor the responsiveness so full and domineering, as Matthew Arnold declared was the condition in England. Did not he say forty years and more ago that the highest classes were sensualized, the middle classes materialized, and the lowest classes brutalized? No such wholesale interpretation or condemnation should be meted out to American society.

The worship of things, however, is too constant and too intense. Yet in this worst dwells the best. The ideals of millions of people are of the noblest type, and the spirit of idealism bathes the communal thinking. In no country is the force for world-wide Christian missions so strong, or the methods for promoting them more wise, or the motives in their propagation more noble. If America is too Chauvinistic, as most countries are, it is also a lover and a benefactor of the world. If it declines to become a member of the League of Nations, and largely, be it added, for political reasons, yet it does send out its best men and women for the service of all nations. If it is inclined to be crass in its luxuries, it is also led to equip relief expeditions and to give millions upon millions of money for those who suffer from pestilence, earthquake, or famine. From materialistic evils it feels the duty of drawing spiritual values.

Under the social category of the best and the worst is found one further item. It relates to the presence of a thoughtful group in the community, small in numbers yet of recognized eminence, and also to the contemporaneous presence of a thoughtless group, large in numbers and powerful in many relations. This duplex fact is one of the results and one of the tokens of democracy at once social and political. The thoughtful group (small) is said by some to be growing smaller. Its first-rate intellects are, as in most communities of the whole world, few. Its geographical center has been, and perhaps still is, found in Cambridge and Boston. A half-century or more ago a visitor from another continent coming to the American would ask to see our noblest. To whom, in answer to his request, would he have been taken? Would he not pay a visit to the Boston historians, to the Cambridge poets, and to the Concord essayists? Would he not go to Elmwood, to the historic house in Brattle Street, to the colonial home on the edge of the Concord meadows? Coming today, to whom, in answer to his repeated request, would he be taken? Perhaps he would not come to either side of the Charles River at all. Perhaps he would be content with visiting various boards at 61 Broadway or 522 Fifth Avenue. Each and all of these boards and corporations were founded by and are manned by great men. Their beneficences go out, on the twin wings of intelligence and of mercy, to all parts of the world. But be it at once said that these foundations are of a type quite unlike the great personalities to whom he would have paid his respects a half-century earlier.

The fact is that America has passed over into the age of a devotion of its best intellects to industrial administration and to the development of material forces. With this change the intellectual concerns of the people have become less purely intellectual and more practically intellectual. With the making of this transfer has gone along a change in the type of the books which are read, of the amusements which are offered and shared in, of the sports which are followed, of the fine arts which are enjoyed. The sober book of scholarship is less often published, and if published is frequently published at the author's expense. The novel sells into the hundreds of thousands of copies. Amusements are cheap in two senses. The dominance of sports is proved by the pages of reports of contests and of games found in the daily journals. The fine arts are represented in free verse, in jazz music, in higgledy-piggledy architecture, in cubist pictures, and in irregular —in more than one sense—dances.

Another element of the social classification of the best and the worst touches the use of leisure. Leisure is a new product in and for America. The class having leisure has rapidly increased in numbers and in impressiveness. This rapid increase is one of the results of a likewise rapid increase of wealth. The use which American society makes of the new gift, or creature, or victim, represents both the best and the worst. One part of society makes a use which results in the betterment of American and of the whole world's life. This use covers great philanthropic, educational, religious, and fundamental political and public undertakings. Such undertakings seem to be numberless as well as diverse. The demands they make are also commanding. Thousands of men and women in America are giving largely of their intellect, of their conscience, and of their will, as well as of their wealth, to these human, humane, and humanistic concerns. I could actually name hundreds of them. God be praised that America has no monopoly of such public servants and benefactors: "Men renowned for their power, giving counsel by their understanding, and declaring prophecies: Leaders of the people by their counsels, and by their knowledge of learning, meet for the people, wise and eloquent in their instructions: . . . honoured in their generations, . . . the glory of their times."[5]

But also there are those who do not make such a use of their newly-found leisure. This use is not so immediately and directly bad as it is futile, empty, aimless, vapid. It is, however, to be added that such leisure may lead to the bad and the bad to the worst. On the part of many men such leisure is devoted to empty talking, to professional idleness, to the making of sport a business—and a not too serious one—to changes of residences and of habits, according to the annual heats and chills, to card-playing, over stakes small as well as large, to flirtations silly, and not always silly, to autoing in which also the swiftness of the machine is in inverse proportion to the intellectual movements. Among women this use of leisure takes on excessive attention to the details of housekeeping, not of homemaking, to the constant problem of clothes, to excessive card-playing, to the carrying-on of an elaborate social *ménage* not confined to one State, but spread out, in latitudes and longitudes, from the Adirondacks to Palm Beach, from New York to Pasadena. Such a life represents an expenditure of money, too, which quite takes the breath away, and which also gives long-drawn sighs for the breath taken away.

From the social relation I now pass to the political. Herein, too, are found impressive illustrations of the best and of the worst.

[5] Ecclesiasticus, xliv.

The federal system of government is the greatest political asset of the American commonwealth. It is, in fact, the most important contribution which this commonwealth has made, or is making, to modern political civilization. It unites the advantages of the small State, the advantages of social and civil equality, of orderly manners, of personal sympathies, of intellectual understandings, with the advantages of the large State, of imperial power, of the rational hope of progressiveness, of commanding the respect of other Governments and the esteem of other peoples. In fact, the federal system, or synthesis, is the only system under which a union of more than a hundred million people can exist in orderliness and in security. Democracy installed as democracy in a hundred million would spell congestion, congestion would create confusion, confusion would eventuate in a permanent mob, and a mob would lead—in the return of the governmental circle—to dictatorship. The federal system has worked well, well fundamentally, and, some would add, well superficially.

The federal system, and many of the forty-eight States which constitute it, are now, in my judgment, beset with the danger of the lessened ability of the members of its law-making bodies. By common confession the intellectual power of the representatives and of the senators was seldom, if ever, of a lower order. Narrowness of intellectual vision obtains. Limitations of political understanding prevails. Selfishness, partisan or personal, seems to be an atmosphere. Altruism, either intellectual or emotional, is remote. The remark of the Swedish statesman, fittingly changed, may be aptly applied: "See with how little wisdom the United States is governed!" The reasons are manifold. Among them are:—First, the most thoughtful and energetic members of the community seem to have concerns more interesting and more commanding than their government. Second, participation in politics as a profession demands wealth, or at least a competency, greater than most possess. Third, to stand for a governmental election represents a campaign of greater strenuousness and is more open to personal assault on reputation and conduct than many are willing to endure. Fourth, the uncertainty of the lasting loyalty of the electorate. Fifth, the small pecuniary compensation, hardly permitting a proper living. (The recent increase from the annual salary of seventy-five hundred dollars to ten thousand dollars for members of Congress does give, however, a certain relief.) Sixth, the actual boredom of many details of the office. Seventh, the lessened importance of the position of a legislator by reason of the increased importance of the executive side of government, and also by reason of the emergence of a rather new method of government through commissions. Eighth, the vanishing place of the strong independent in politics, and the enlarged and very dominant place of the party system. Ninth, the breakdown of the two-party system and the creation of the three-party, giving lessened hope of the success of aggressive movements for public welfare. Tenth, the influence of the uncultured, narrow-minded, vociferous legislator as greater than the influence of the considerate member, of large-heartedness and broad-mindedness. Eleventh, the difficulty of getting proper legislation by reason of the obstructive rules of the House, and especially of the Senate. Twelfth, the diminishing hope of the improvement of society by government, and the strengthening of the hope of improvement through social forces. For these and other reasons many of the best citizens decline to stand for a Congressional nomination even if asked, and, of course, few are asked.

In the same political field, and also in the social, the problem of taxation easily represents both the best and the worst. The problem is one which arises from people living together in large numbers and in close relationships. The rural population has fallen to forty, and the urban has increased to sixty, per cent. As the number living in cities increases, and as the relations become more intimate, the cost of such habitation enlarges. The rise in cost is an inevitable consequence. It is a consequence which citizens accept with a certain degree of dissatisfaction and of grumbling. Yet they prefer acceptance to rural segregations. The close communal relationship forms, historically as well as immediately, one of the best and one of the worst conditions and results of American and other national life.

But this result, as I have intimated, entails a heavy, and an increasingly heavy, cost. This cost is of two kinds. The formal Government is constantly beset by the problem of getting money for these heavy and heavier costs. It therefore seeks to devise new methods with closer inquisitiveness, and to work old ones with greater forcefulness. Increased import duties, taxes on large gifts— even to charity—on incomes represent the new means and methods. The more complete listing of all properties, and the more complete details of income of all kinds, real and personal, are constantly and rather severely demanded. The penalties for failures in making the required returns become more inevitable and severe.

Yet, in addition to such formal taxes, taxes which might be called informal, become more commanding. By such informal taxes I mean the contributions which are requested, and which are at times almost demanded, from rich or well-to-do citizens for the relief of poverty, for the rehabilitation of fallen families, for the foundation of orphanages, for the establishment and administration of homes for the aged, for the building and support of hospitals, and for the endowment of colleges and universities: Such institutions and agencies are carried forward on the informal tax budgets of the whole community. Such methods, such forces, and such results represent the best service of the community. The necessity of supporting them creates one of the most Christian and altruistic of all forms of public endeavor. But the cost of such beneficence and administration does constitute a burden which the community is finding very hard to bear.

To one other of the more recondite of the conditions—political, social, and economic—before passing on to the next section I wish to allude. The American Federal and State Governments, like most of the older Governments of the world, were set up as a political and civil machine; for the relation of the people to the Government was largely political and civil. But, within a hundred years, to these relations have been added two others, social and economic. Without accepting or seeking for fundamental changes in government, the American people are applying an old political machine to new sets of conditions. They are finding that the application results in all sorts of miscarriages. Many questions, therefore, emerge to the serious mind. Chiefly among them are these or this: Should a new social and economic machine be established for controlling and guiding social and economic forces, or should the American people seek to adapt the old political and civil forms of government to the new conditions, social and economic? The question I ask, and simply ask. I must now be content with asking, without attempting any answer.

It is easy and natural to pass from the social and political condition to the educational. Herein are also found the best and the worst, and the two are also found lying close together.

The best element in any education today in America is research. It is found primarily lodged in the college and university, but it may also be found in many an industrial plant and private laboratory. It is the most beneficent of all the offerings which the German university in the American-German educational period of a hundred years has given. It applies to all fields of knowledge or of ignorance. Whether its arrow is tipped with a very humane and philanthropic purpose, or whether it represents what the great Benjamin Peirce in a college lecture once said of a certain equation, "Thank God, that can serve no human purpose," the movement is fundamental and, be it added, splendid. It touches not the narrow and ephemeral. It touches the cubical and lasting relations of all existence. It represents patient and long-continued, far-flung understandings on the part of the investigator. It demands for him freedom, leisure, proper material, environment, and personal coöperativeness. It requires books and other apparatus and opportunities for timely and fitting publication. It may or it may not be coördinated with teaching in the university. If so coördinated, it should be found as a quickening force to teaching, and teaching in turn, should not delay its proper progress, or subtract from its splendid consummations. Failure in winning a presumed result, or in making an anticipated discovery, should not be suffered to interfere with the general conclusion of its value. The finding of unexpected truths, and most important ones too, as so often occurs, should give renewed incentive to the investigator's quest. The most recent discoveries in the germs of typhoid, of scarlet fever and of tuberculosis, as well as the earlier discoveries in diphtheria, should give, and do give, quickening to the forces working for the conquest of other fields of life or of death. Biochemists and biophysicists standing by their laboratory tables; astronomers gazing through incomprehensible distances into the light of new suns; psychologists, psychiatrists, historians, and Oriental archæologists, all are alike toiling by day or by night, by year or by decade, in learning and in interpreting truth. The Harvard shield of *Veritas* and the Yale of *Lux et Veritas* are the quickening mottoes of the researches in all universities and graduate schools. The knowledge gained and to be gained by man, of man, and of all that concerns man, is the best force and the highest value in American education. The diversity and breadth of this field are intimated in the fact that at an annual meeting of a limited society, namely, the American Society of Anatomists, there were reported more than a hundred pieces of research, undertaken or pursued within a few months. A report of similar significance could be made of the

American Medical Association, of the Chemical Society, and above all, of the American Association for the Advancement of Science.

But with this best is linked also the worst. The first element in this worst is superficiality. In no respect is the contrast between the American and the German people more fundamental than is found in the thoroughness of the one and the superficiality of the other in scholastic concerns. Of course each quality has its degrees. The German goes down deep, but does not go out broad. The American goes out broad, and does not go down deep. The German student says, "I want to go down into this thing." The American says, "I must get on and get up!" The one includes relations complex: the other is direct and thin. The German student considers too few subjects; he is guilty of narrowness. The American embraces too many; he is guilty of thinness. The German student says *multum;* the American student's motto is *multa.*

A second elemental weakness grows out of the first. It is the emphasis laid on the vocational, or even pre-vocational, part of education. The liberal type is sacrificed to the professional or to the practical. The advancement made in thirty or more years in a few medical and law schools in regarding an academic education as necessary to the undertaking of professional study is in peril of being vitiated. The harm is wrought by bringing back professional studies into the college of liberal learning. The cause of this backwater movement is found largely in the introduction of the "specialities" into the later years of the medical school. The peril lies, first, in sacrificing the liberal education to the refinements of professional training, and, secondly, in making the college a business school. For, be it added, more than one-half of the graduates of colleges, like Harvard, Yale, and Princton, pass at once from their commencement platforms to brokers' or other offices and to woollen, cotton, or other factories.

One cause of the early introduction of professional studies into the undergraduate curriculum lies in the proper desire to shorten, or at least not to lengthen out, the whole educational course. The recent lengthening of this course applies especially to the medical school and profession. For the physician under present conditions and methods is not able to begin his professional career before the age of twenty-seven. So late a beginning does not make for his happiness either personal or professional, or for the welfare of the community.

The third form of our educational badness lies in a somewhat different plane. It relates to a fundamental weakness in the teaching process itself. It touches the method of teaching found in conveying information instead of in quickening unto vigorous thought and alert, logical thinking. Teaching is prone to emphasize the fact, the single fact, which is of course good. It is liable to neglect relating fact to fact and the inferring of a new truth, which is better. It is in danger of passing over the law of causality. If it does not omit the method of analysis in intellectual discipline, which it is liable to do, it yet neglects, more and most, the difficult duty of emphasizing properly the law of synthesis. To the information which is easy to give and to acquire, and which is indeed important, it is more important to add inspiration, and to inspiration it is yet more and most important to add edification, which is most difficult. The teaching in the American high school or academy is much inferior to the teaching in the English public school, as the teaching in the typical American college, in its effect on intellectual character, is inferior to the tutorial system of Oxford and of Cambridge.

In any survey of the best and the worst in America, mention should be made of literature and of what literature connotes.

The best in American literature is found in its historians and poets. An addition to these two classes should at once be made of its essayists and of its novelists. But these additions contain only one name each. The best literature of the colonial period was historical, likewise of the middle period of the nineteenth century. In the list of historians of the middle period are included six names: Henry C. Lea, Henry Adams, Parkman, Prescott, Motley, Bancroft. Lea chose a remote and mediæval period. In it he was a master. Lord Bryce once said to me that Lea was the best of the American historians. Adams selected a short period, one identified with his own great family. Parkman crossed over into Canada, selected several episodes, and wrote of them in fullness, with picturesqueness and in a spirit of affection. Prescott and Motley, like Lea, went far afield, into Central and South America and into Holland, writing volumes which apparently will live, despite the fuller investigations into earlier American civilizations. Bancroft, of many relations, through forty years devoted himself, in ten volumes, to interpreting the history of his own country. This American sextette takes its place with a not dissimilar sextette which, omitting Gibbon, might be formed of English historians. Of the poets, Lowell represents the most thoughtful and fundamentally quickening. His *Commemoration Ode* is his noblest contribution. Longfellow still sings sweet songs for the multitude, cheering the sorrowing heart, giving reinforcements to the tempted conscience and new power to the flagging will. More than six hundred pieces of music have been written to interpret his verses. In poetry, however, the contribution is far less rich than in history. In the essay, be it added, or the novel the offering is still meager. In the essay the outstanding figure is, of course, Emerson, and in romance Hawthorne. If space permitted, it would not be difficult to draw analogies between the poverties of American and the richness of English literature, as it would be easy to draw a not unlike contrast between Latin literature and Greek.

The American is the maker, and the reader, rather of papers than of books, these papers being first daily, or even hourly. He reads, and makes also, daily papers before the weekly, and the weekly before the monthly magazine, and the monthly magazine before he makes or reads the quarterlies. His daily papers he reads also in flamboyant headlines which appeal to his emotions or capacity for sensations. The dominance rather of the emotional than of the intellectual in the American mind finds no more striking illustration than in its newspaper preferences. Of course, too, the newspaper has a rival in the moving picture or cinema, of the life of the month, of the adventures of the week, of the casualties of the day or of the hour. These pictures, too, include the doings of the world and are of a type of the world's doings to a degree which, to the thoughtful students of the human drama, is either sad or disgusting or both sad and disgusting.

There is one further element connected with literature which is noteworthy in its historical or present relations. The American prefers spoken to written literature. He would rather hear the speaker than read the writer. His choice, too, is of the flamboyant, emotional type rather than of the sober, thoughtful, contemplative. The form of the speaking of the House of Commons makes to him slight appeal. The form of speaking of the colored preacher also makes slight appeal. But between the two extremes talk which is directed primarily to the emotions, and secondly to the intellect, moves him most, and is by him preferred. Of course, as intelligence rises, the intellectual type of speaking becomes the more dominant and the more acceptable. As feelings rise, the emotional type takes on a stronger and inevitable appeal.

The sixth, and the last, of the American fields in which I seek for the best and the worst is that most important one of religion. In this field are at least three parts of the best and not less than four parts of the worst.

The first part of the best is interpreted by the all-embracing word "liberty." As applied to religion, liberty represents largely what it is found to represent when applied to the individual. Religious life in the individual, or in an association of individuals, is free in its beliefs and in the manifestation of its beliefs. No doctrine however illogical, no dogma however irrational, no manifestation of emotion however silly, no practice however trifling, is denied to the citizen. Doctrines and dogmas, manifestations and practices, in their lack of logic and of reason and in their possession of the silly and the trivial, are stretched to their extremes. But the formal law and the customary permit such eccentricities. Bad as eccentricities are, any attempt to interfere with them would be far worse. The freedom seems to be somewhat of a rescript of the apparent method of the Divine Government in dealing with the will of man. Terrible as may be the results of both methods, any attempt at restraint would necessarily give results yet more terrible—more terrible for the development of the individual and of the race.

The second section of the best in religion relates to the æsthetic appeal which classical architecture and noble music are making to the sense of worship and of devotion. A somewhat new element is herein found. For one does not forget the Puritan and the Pilgrim foundation of the American Church and of American society. But within the last generation an appreciation of Gothic architecture and of great compositions in music has developed. The new cathedrals in Washington and in New York are illustrations of the one, and the noble renderings of the noblest oratorios by great choruses heard in the large cities of the other. The worshipful element in the building of cathedrals of the historic type has indeed developed far faster than has the rational element. The reason, I apprehend, is found in at least three conditions: (*a*) The increase of wealth, which permits and invites increase of æsthetic expenditure. (*b*) The weariness of the American mind and heart, consequent upon the keener competitions of professional and business struggle. That mind, therefore, longs for the spirit of restfulness in worship, even in the loss of a certain satisfaction in intellectual meanings and discussion. (*c*) The general enlargement and enrichment of the appreciation of the people for the sublime and the beautiful. The early crudeness and barbarities are passing. The whole world is offering its holiest in the ecclesiastical fine arts to that part of itself which is called the New World.

A third element of the **religious** best lies in what may be called the foreign missionary movement. This movement began as a distinct evangelistic endeavor, a little more than a hundred years ago, in two academic groups at Williamstown and at Andover. It has constantly enlarged its ongoings. Its vision of the world, a world interpreted as pagan or half-heathen, has become ethical while still remaining evangelical. In the united ethical and evangelical service it has also become intellectually educational. It has been indeed "instant in season and out of season" in preaching the Word. But it has also founded colleges in China, Japan, India, and Turkey, established kindergartens in Kobe and Bombay, endowed medical schools and hospitals in Peking and Tokio, invented power-looms for the weaving of Indian cloths, and opened health clinics in the slum districts of a score of national capitals. Of Christ's two consummate commandments, without disobeying the first, it has practiced, and practices, the second.

Hard by these three elements of the best lie other elements which are not the best. Of them I wish to point out four.

The first of these is found in the divisions of the Protestant Church. These formal divisions number no less than one hundred and sixty-eight. The robe of Christ has been cut up into many parts. Its wholeness has become shreds. The causes of the divisions run from principles which are fundamental in human nature to inferences and emphases and implications which are silly, trivial, transient in time, and narrow in relationship. In consequence the Churches are rivals for the loyalty and support of the people. Especially in the rural districts, denominational competitions are keen. Ecclesiastical individualisms should result, in the final analysis, in the mutual strengthening and co-working of all Churches. In the country parts of America they do result, on the contrary, in mutual disintegration. At least, the building up of one Church is often secured by the tearing down of others.

But be it gratefully said that such disintegrations are becoming less common and less disastrous. The fundamental and catholic bases of faith are now more fully recognized. The wisdom of large and just policies is generally understood and assented to by ecclesiastical governing boards and by individual societies. The signal evidence of such an agreement is found in the Federal Council of the Churches of Christ in America, an organization established about a decade ago, and now comprising no less than twenty-eight of the great denominational bodies. Its service touches fields as diverse as education, international justice and good-will, and relations of the races. It is concerned with the Churches of Europe and with those of the Near and the Far East. Greatly manned and well equipped, it bears promise of becoming a vital, uniting, and integrating force.

A second bad part of American religion is its ignorant emotionalism. Emotionalism with the "ism" is as evil as proper emotion itself is good. When to emotionalism is prefixed ignorance, as it usually is prefixed, the result is rather disastrous. Be it said, too, that the evil of emotionalism can well be measured by its accompanying ignorance. Of course, such a condition is found preëminent in the colored race. In utterances which are ridiculous, in elocutions which are hollerings, in responses to prayers which make the irreverent laugh and the reverent hearer grieve, in movements of body which indicate that one has got the "power," are these ignorances and emotions incorporated. But extravagances and eccentricities are not confined to the practices of a single race. They are found on the northern Mississippi prairie and the Rocky Mountain slopes, as well as in the bayous of Louisiana and the mountains of Tennessee. They represent an absence of self-knowledge and a lack of self-control which, if not a form of insanity, are at least a form of inanity, and do, at all events, approach the level of barbarity.

Quite remote from such communal or individual eccentricities is yet another weakness. It is the absence of the religious training in the individual home. The era in which the husband and father was the priest at his own domestic altar has passed. There is no altar and the priest has put aside his vestments. Prayers each morning in the typical family are no longer offered. The daily reading of the Bible has ceased to be a custom. The blessing at the family meal is said only when the pastor is bidden as a guest. The religious education of children by parents is sorely neglected. The American child is growing up without a knowledge of the Bible as either a noble piece of literature or as an instrument of personal devotion and worship. I have tested the knowledge of college students in respect to the Scriptures, and I have found their knowledge ignorance. Character, based on the Bible as history, as poetry, as biography, as ethics, as religion, is neglected in the American home. Religion, therefore, suffers in its very foundation and origin. The results are at once lamentable to society, as they are disintegrating or hardening to the individual.

As I read over these sheets two comprehensive inferences spring to the mind.

One is that American society and life, in the best elements, represent relations strong and enriching in the highest forces. The best is becoming better, and to each increment of good is added a yet further comparative and superlative. The white is taking on a whiteness yet more splendid. Contrariwise, at the bottom is found a worst which is becoming yet worse. The black is taking on a deeper blackness. The slums are growing more slum-like. The criminal class is becoming more criminal in both numbers and evil.

A further comprehensive inference is both a good and a bad, both a best and a worst. Sir Henry Sumner Maine says in his *Ancient Law:* "If then we employ Status, agreeably with the usage of the best writers, to signify these personal conditions only, and avoid applying the term to such conditions as are the immediate or remote result of agreement, we may say that the movement of the progressive societies has hitherto been a movement *from Status to Contract.*"[6] The reaction, however, has begun. Contract still rules. It is most benevolent and beneficent. But the wave has turned. Status, signifying "personal conditions only," has again become a ruling force for both evil and for good, for both the best and the worst in America.

[6] P. 165.

II

THE AMERICAN FAMILY *

THE place which the family occupies as a social unit has, in the last fifty years, distinctly narrowed. The lessened worth of the family, as a social unit, may be interpreted by reference to the current doubt regarding the happiness which the family creates and conserves. For much doubt is expressed regarding the happiness of the American home. Ask, even at a wedding, the ordinary guest whether there are more happy than unhappy marriages, and the answer will likely be that the unhappy marriages exceed the happy. Whatever might prove to be the truth—if the truth it were possible to learn,—the simple fact that the belief is as it is, is significant. The belief or doubt of one individual regarding the happiness or unhappiness of the American home may be only a reflection of the personal conjugal condition of the one speaking. An answer, too, might be based more upon observation than upon experience. But I believe that the supposition is quite rife that the marriage which is distinctly happy is exceptional. I, for one, do not believe

* July, 1911.

that the distinctly happy marriage is exceptional, but the supposition is so common as-to awaken serious foreboding.

The interpreter of social and domestic phenomena may justly comment upon this condition by saying that such a conclusion belongs to the progress of all affairs human. Such a conclusion marks the movement from youth to age, from a noble and hopeful promise to imperfect fulfillment. The condition is not unique. What merchant gets the wealth he anticipated? What lawyer secures the practice which he believed was assured? What doctor is as useful to the community as he thought he would be? What minister serves the people as nobly as he anticipated? The promise of the dawn of life and of career is not usually made good in the afternoon. The condition, therefore, of marital unhappiness should not be charged up as a debt against the family, but rather should be interpreted as a condition of human character and service.

The moralist may also be permitted to say that happiness is no more the supreme purpose of the family than it is the supreme purpose of the individual. Epicureanism, however highly refined or broadly conceived, does not represent the final cause of the building of domestic altars. The enlargement and enrichment of personality, the proper training of children, the performance of the duty owed to general society in making contributions for its betterment, represent the causes of the foundation and of the continuance of the family far more important than is the happiness of the family. Therefore, even if the family has failed to secure happiness, it has not necessarily failed to secure advantages of far greater worth.

But the philosopher might be allowed to say that the home which is not happy is seldom able to make any worthy contribution to the social wealth of the community. It is not able, usually, to give a proper training to children. It also commonly serves to narrow and to deplete, to render acrid or bitter the personality of its older members. Happiness may be an unworthy purpose for the foundation and continuance of the home, but happiness seems to be a necessary condition for the home to secure results which are more precious than happiness. Happiness is the soil in which the flowers of the gentle ministry of love, of self-sacrifice, of enriched and beautiful personality come to their sweetest blooming.

But I venture to believe that most homes are less unhappy than the current interpretation judges them to be. And I also believe that the number of homes which are unhappy is less large than commonly thought. Even if there be one divorce for some six marriages, or fewer, as is the fact in the State of Indiana, in certain years, it is not to be forgotten that there are six marriages for only one divorce. Divorce is still exceptional. It is also to be borne in mind that reports of domestic happiness do not get into the newspapers. The reporter's pencil has no affinity for the happy home. The happy home is quiet and orderly. Certain types of domestic infelicity and irregularity are anything but quiet and orderly. They are blatant and hysterical. For them the reporter's pencil has a distinct and immediate affinity. The ideal of a happy home is, I believe, more constantly and more fully realized than are the ideals entertained in youth of obtaining wealth or fame or any other form of what is called success. Have we a right to put on the home a unique and exceptional demand for the realization of its dreams? For the home does not stand alone as a social institution. It is constituted by individuals. It bears the impress of their character. It is placed in the social order and environment; it is touched by this environment, invested by this order. It in turn helps to form the personalities which constitute and continue to maintain it, and it also in turn aids in the promotion of the social welfare. On the whole is it not true that the home is finer in sentiment, richer in noble feeling, more worthily self-contained and more nobly successful in securing the supreme ends of humanity, than are the single persons who form the home or who make social relations which constitute its environment?

But although all this may be true, it is nevertheless also true that the home has in these last years suffered a decline as the source and center of the best life. The causes of this decline, occurring in recent years, go back into time not recent. The causes go back into the Protestant Reformation.

The Protestant Reformation was the greatest movement for individualism in human society which the world has ever known. It was not simply a religious movement; it was not merely a protest against ecclesiasticism; but, though the movement was aimed directly at ecclesiasticism, through ecclesiasticism it was a movement aimed at the freedom of the individual life. It was a protest against domination over the personal intellect, over the personal will, or over the personal spiritual life. It resulted in the elevation of the individual heart and mind as against the sentiment and faith universal and Catholic. It substituted the judgment of the individual for the judgment of a hierarchy. The Reformation and the Renaissance united to give a new spirit of liberty and of culture, and this spirit of liberty and culture touched individuals as well as institutions. Both the Renaissance and the Reformation have resulted in the elevation of the individual and the decline of the family as a social unit. The distribution of the Bible in the vernacular gave the German and the English people the most advanced opportunity in recent centuries of emphasizing the right of private judgment and the responsibility of each man for his intellectual and moral character. The advent and the spread of the Puritan idea emphasized the personality of each person. Bacon and the Cartesian philosophers impressed the duty of each man to search out the truth for himself. In poem and tractate Milton pleaded for the liberty of the individual. Locke, indirectly through his sensational philosophy, and directly through his essays on government, placed the single man and not a dogmatic system as the center of social and legal order. The French philosophers of the middle of the eighteenth century, and especially Rousseau, followed the earlier English metaphysicians in their tendency to elevate the individual above social institutions. Transferred to the new world, the individualism of the Renaissance and of the Reformation flowered into a political democracy, and a political democracy in turn developed a more intense form of individualism. The political principle upon which was waged the contest of the American colonies for independence—that government derives its just powers from the consent of the governed—was the development of the social principle of the supremacy of the individual. The affirmation of the Declaration of Independence that all men are created equal was simply the application of a current French notion of the equality of individuals, as the assertion of the inalienable right of liberty was simply the application of a current English notion of individual freedom. This theory the French Revolution stretched to such a length that it broke into pieces. The American Revolution so conserved the theory that it built on it the State and the social order.

It cannot for an instant be doubted that the advent and development of individualism have contributed to the decline of the home as a social unit and force. The historic progress and movement are evident, but the potency of other forces now existing, contributing to a similar result, is no less real and forceful.

Education, moreover, in its lower and higher ranges, has come to be the dominant force in modern American life. Through the public school and private, through the university and the college, either endowed from public funds or by private beneficence, are created the strongest force of our age by which the State primarily seeks its own conservation. The State may and does, through various tests, determine what class of men shall, as lawyers, or as practitioners of medicine or of dentistry, be regarded as capable of caring for important interests of the commonwealth. But the State makes no attempt to require a professional education of a certain number of citizens, yet the State does absolutely determine that every child shall, for a certain number of weeks of each year and for certain years of his life, attend the public or other school. The teacher, therefore, represents the most significant force of the civil power. But education, be it remembered, is a matter in, of, and for the individual: The education of the primary school and of the university seeks to train the individual in that most important principle discovered or applied in the realm of education of the last fifty years, known as the elective principle. The elective principle is based simply and only upon the character of the individual. In education the family and the school exist for the individual; and it is only in relations other than educational that the individuals exist for the family and for the State. The presence, therefore, of education, as the most potent of all social forces, has resulted in the appreciation of individualism and in the depreciation of the family.

Modern life, too, has contributed toward a similar result through its enlargement. For modern life has vastly enlarged the sphere of the individual. Each individual is or may be a world-citizen. Wherever he lives, in hamlet or metropolis, in prairie village or in national capital, he may know the world. The newspaper each day offers him the news of Australia, Sweden, South Africa, and Brazil. His table is spread with food gathered from Texas, from the wheat-fields of the northwest, from the orange groves of California and of Florida, and from the banana trees of the Tropics. The famines of India are of interest to him, and the revolutions in China or Turkey make direct appeals to his enthusiasms or indignations. These knowledges and conditions represent an increase of interest in things outside the home, and help to explain the decline of interest in things inside the home. But be it remembered that these interests are the interests of the individual. Such interests, thus organized and constituted, result in the narrowing of the home as a center of life.

I do not doubt, moreover, that the great independence of woman, constantly growing in the last fifty years, has resulted in a decline of interest on the part of women in the life of the family. The sphere of her activities has enlarged, and these activities themselves have become more significant. Seventy-five years ago the household and the schoolhouse were the two hemispheres in which women could fittingly work; today in almost every business and profession women are engaged. What woman does not do is far easier to indicate than what she does attempt. The whole movement known as "Woman's Rights" is specially significant. This movement was, and is, in many ways nothing less than superb. In many respects it has on its side all the virtues, the veracities, and the verities. But be it said clearly and emphatically it was, and is, a movement for and of individualism. It was, and is, a movement to give to the women of the family certain presumed rights and opportunities and to impose on them certain duties and obligations which the men of the family had formerly exercised or performed. I am not saying but that this movement is, on the whole, wise and most beneficent; but I do say that the movement has resulted in a prominence of individualism which has, at least indirectly, resulted in the subordination of the family.

To yet one more cause of the decline of the importance of the family in recent times I wish to allude. This cause I shall call a decline in the sense of social or conjugal duty. The sense of industrial duty has, I think, distinctly lessened in the last decade. The ordinary workman at his trade does not take that interest in his work which he formerly took. The æsthetic and ethical sense of doing his job well has suffered. A similar decline is evident in respect to the family. Both men and women are less inclined to regard marriage as a duty than in the earlier time. The single life is, for most people, and especially for men, easier than the married life. The married life, in the duties which it imposes on each member of the pair, who constitute this life, respecting, in particular, the proper rearing of children, is a life of many and serious responsibilities. The joys of life are magnified, made more rich and ennobling, but the obligations of the life are made correspondingly binding and serious. From the assuming of such obligations many persons conscientiously shrink. They prefer to offer their contribution to human force through the independent work of the office rather than through the dependent work of the home. The unwillingness, therefore, to assume certain duties, serious for the individual, serious for the home, and serious for society, represents a relative decline of the family.

By reason of these causes—the individualizing force of the Protestant Reformation, enlarged education, the complexity of modern life, the lessening of the sense of social or conjugal duty—the value of the family, as a social unit, has suffered a great decline. A man who wills or works for the betterment of the race cannot but sorrow over such a decline.

The position now occupied by the family is indeed far higher than that occupied by the Jewish family in the time of Christ, or by the Greek or Roman family in the first Christian century, but the position in the United States is lower than it has been in two hundred and fifty years. In social, religious, ethical, and personal value it is still great, but the value is less great than it has been at any period.

The purpose is, therefore, made evident and obligatory of the restoration of the family. In the securing of this purpose I wish to point out certain methods.

A stricter and more constant use should be made of what may be called the legal sanctions for the establishment of the family. These legal sanctions are of the simplest sort. They arise from the relation of the family to the social order. This social order has an interest in the establishment of each home. Therefore marriage is not to be regarded as an affair of simply two individuals. It has relation to society and to humanity. Publicity, therefore, should attend the solemnization of every marriage. In order, furthermore, to give assurance of the fitness of marriage in and to the social order, its solemnization should represent forethought and deliberation. It were well if not a day, as is the law in most States, but if at least a week should intervene between the authority of the State giving consent to the solemnization of marriage and the solemnization itself. Moreover, it were well to do away with what is now known as common-law marriage. Such a recognition, in some instances, may result in the relief of certain contracting parties, but, in general, the law creates more abuses than it relieves.

The family, also, should receive the support of what I shall call social distinction. Its members should determine that its place in the social order should be great. Knowing that the destruction of the family aids in the disintegration of the general social bond which constitutes society, its members should labor for its perpetuity. The home may be called, adopting the terms of biology, the social cell. Society from this cell is created. Every part, therefore, should be made to maintain the integrity and to promote the progress of this primary social force. At this point, the joint will of the two members which essentially constitute the home has the greatest value. Every home may be maintained if the members will to maintain it. Any home may be destroyed if either of the two members wills to destroy it.

The third support in the restoration of the home to its proper place and function is found in what may be called the domestic sanctions.

These sanctions are constituted largely by the children of a marriage. The stress and strain, to which the conjugal tie is subjected when that tie alone unites a husband and a wife, is great. The stress and strain to which the conjugal tie is subjected when that tie unites not only a husband and wife but also children, is yet greater than when it unites husband and wife only; but be it said with firmer emphasis that the strength of the tie itself is increased by far greater strength than is the stress and strain increased through the presence of children. If one should say that marriage is framed for the sake of children, it is also true to say that children are created for the sake of the perpetuity of the wedlock, out of which they spring.

Advancing civilizations are in peril of becoming declining social stages by reason of a diminished birth-rate. The diminished birth-rate obtaining in France and in the early native stock of the United States is the cause of public lamentation. This diminished birth-rate is more conspicuous in families of the Protestant than of the Roman Catholic faith. The blessing of the Roman Catholic priesthood upon a numerous progeny is more abounding than that obtaining among the adherents of the Protestant religion.

The lack of children among what are known as the educated classes is most evident. In the six classes of Harvard College from 1872 to 1877 inclusive, 634 members had at a recent date married.

In 1902 the surviving children of these marriages numbered 1,262—that is to say, the members of the classes who have married, together with their wives, have just practically reproduced themselves; or when one considers that 28 per cent. of the members of these six classes are not married, it is evident that the educated people do not reproduce themselves. This condition obtaining in recent years at Harvard College is not unique. For at Wesleyan University, Connecticut, the average number of children to each marriage from 1833 to 1840 was 4.5. In the decade from 1841 to 1850 it was 3.3; in the decade from 1851 to 1860 it was 3.2, and in the decade from 1861 to 1870 it was 2.6. The average number of children for each graduate, not for each marriage, in this same decade was 2.4. For the four decades under review the number of children for each marriage was 3.4. The current lamentation regarding the small size of the better American family is in part reasonable and in part unreasonable. The American family should, under ordinary conditions, perpetuate or more than perpetuate itself. The ordinary family should also bear children, in order to secure not only its perpetuity but also its integrity. The number of children, however, born to a family is of less consequence than that there should be children born to the family. The personal responsibilities which parents assume in bringing children into the world are so great that they should not become fathers and mothers unless they are ready to bear these responsibilities willingly. It is also to be remembered that the highest happiness of the family in and for itself may be, to a degree, sacrificed under the power of the procreative impulse.

From the sanctions of religion, moreover, great help should be derived in the conservation of the family. For the family as an individual, religion possesses inherent worth. A marriage which is interpreted as having relation only to the two parties contracting it is in dire peril of dissolution. Marriage which is interpreted as having relation not only to the two parties contracting it, but also to the social order, is in less peril of dissolution; but the marriage which is interpreted as having relationship not only to the two parties contracting it, and to the social order, but also to ultimate being, gives grounds for the strongest assurance of its permanence. From the earliest time religion has contributed to the growth from polygamy and polyandry into monogamy. In certain stages and at certain times the religious interpretation of marriage has been blind or ferocious. In India the religious interpretation has been the cause of hideous abuses; but, on the whole, religion has been the mightiest force making for the highest type of marriage.

It should be said that the Roman Catholic Church has, on the whole, accomplished far more for the perpetuity of the marriage rite and for the integrity of the family than has the Protestant. From that extreme view which the Reformed Confession adopted touching marriage as a civil rite, which became of peculiar significance in the United States, there should be made a vital and fundamental reaction. If the Protestant communicant is not prepared to affirm with the Catholic that marriage is a sacrament, he can, at least, grant that marriage is sacramental. For, as Pope Leo XIII., in an encyclical issued in 1880, said: "For Christ Our Lord raised matrimony to the dignity of a sacrament; and matrimony is the contract itself, provided only that it be lawfully made. In addition to which, matrimony is a sacrament for this reason, that it is a sacred sign conveying grace, and presenting an image of the mystic nuptials of Christ with the Church. But the form and figure of these is expressed by that bond of perfect unity by which man and wife are joined together, and which is nothing else but matrimony itself. Therefore it is evident that every lawful marriage between Christians is in and by itself a sacrament; and nothing can be more opposed to truth than that the sacrament is but an ornamental addition, or a character imparted from without, which may be separated and disjoined from the contract at will.''

It were well if such teaching in essence were adopted by members of the Protestant Churches.

But the help that is of abounding value and of lasting worth in the restoration of the family lies in the personal sanctions. By the personal sanctions are meant the relationship of the two persons who unite themselves in marriage. Whatever may be the worth of the other sanctions, legal, social, domestic, religious, the worth of this simple sanction is greater than the value of all others. The home that is founded on economic marriages, or upon marriages representing social functions and conveniences, or upon passion, is in peril of destruction. Marriages which, in a word, are based on love, give promise, and they alone give promise, of lasting permanence and of noble enrichment. Such domestic unions are spiritual. In them the element of sex is necessary, but from this element the consciousness of sex soon vanishes. Such domestic unions represent unity of heart and intellect, of will and of conscience. Such marriages, moreover, represent the primary element of equality; each member of the union is *par inter pares*. Out of such conditions of spiritual unity and equality permanence is assured. Marriage that is thus based upon love represents the highest state to which a man and woman can attain. Its felicity has been well interpreted by John Stuart Mill. In his book on the subjection of women, Mill says: "What marriage may be in the case of two persons of cultivated faculties, identical in opinions and purposes, between whom there exists that best kind of equality, similarity of powers and capacities with reciprocal superiority in them—so that each can enjoy the luxury of looking up to the other, and can have alternately the pleasure of leading and being led in the path of development—I will not attempt to describe. To those who can conceive it, there is no need; to those who cannot, it would appear the dream of an enthusiast. But I maintain, with the profoundest conviction, that this, and this only, is the ideal of marriage; and that all opinions, customs, and institutions which favour any other notion of it, or turn the conceptions and aspirations connected with it into any other direction, by whatever pretences they may be coloured, are relics of primitive barbarism. The moral regeneration of mankind will only really commence, when the most fundamental of the social relations is placed under the rule of equal justice, and when human beings learn to cultivate their strongest sympathy with an equal in rights and in cultivation."[1]

For the restoration of the family to the place it should occupy in human society, I know of no better methods than those which are embodied in the proper relations of marriage to the civil law, in the increasing of the social obligations embodied in wedlock and family, in the domestic sanctions which marriage imposes, and in the religious duties and opportunities which it represents; but, besides these sanctions, love itself is fundamental. Without it, the other helps for the restoration of the family are of small value.

[1] *The Subjection of Women*, by John Stuart Mill, p. 383 (in volume containing *On Liberty*, and *The Subjection of Women*.)

III

THE PILGRIMS' MOTIVE AND CONTRIBUTION *

INDISCRIMINATE eulogy is as irrational to the judgment as it is unpleasant to the trained emotion. The Mayflower Company is the victim, on its three hundredth anniversary year, of general commendations which are quite as true to the emotional eulogist as they are false to the discriminating historian. For in all the significance of the Pilgrim emigration—significances which one of their sons in the ninth generation would be the last to undervalue—there does appear at least one element which deserves special consideration and which is in peril of not receiving proper proportional emphasis.

This element is the fact that the little company of one hundred and two souls, with a single or partial exception, contained no man of liberal education: searches made in the matriculation registers of Cambridge and of Oxford have failed to reveal a single name of a family or individual of the Mayflower Company, with the exception of that of Elder Brewster. Brewster matriculated at

* October, 1920.

that most ancient college, Peterhouse, at Cambridge, in the year 1580; but he left without receiving a degree. For nine years following the landing he was the only man of university training in the Plymouth Colony. In 1629 Ralph Smith, a matriculant of Christ's College, Cambridge, in or about the year 1612, became the first settled minister and the second member of the Company of liberal education. It was not, be it added, until another period of eight years had passed, in all seventeen years after the landing, that a third addition was made to the duet of so-called educated men.

This fact becomes the more important when it is remembered that to the one hundred and two members of the Mayflower Company were added, in the course of the remaining years of the decade, thirty-five arriving in 1621, sixty arriving in 1623, thirty-five with their families arriving also in the Mayflower in 1629, and sixty who arrived in 1630, making a total of nearly three hundred.

Intellectual relationships and motives were in fact lacking in the Plymouth Colony. It was not until the first generation had passed away that public schools were formally established. It is also significant that among the graduates of Harvard College from 1642, when the first degrees were conferred, down to the year 1658, comprising no less than ninety-seven men, are found the names of only one native and two residents of Plymouth Colony.

This interpretation of the lack of liberally educated men and of educational motives among the citizens of the Plymouth Colony, an interpretation at once so simple and so significant, becomes yet more impressive when it is brought into comparative contrast with a corresponding interpretation of the presence of liberally educated men and with the support of liberal education in the neighboring colony of Massachusetts Bay. In the Bay Colony there were resident about ninety graduates of Cambridge and of Oxford,[1] the larger number coming from Cambridge, and for a reason which will be presently touched upon. Of the Cambridge colleges Emmanuel furnished the larger share, about a score being credited to this Puritan foundation. Among the Emmanuel names I find Thomas Hooker, John Cotton, Nathaniel Ward, Thomas Shepard, and John Harvard; Trinity, Cambridge, furnished the next larger number. In the list I find the names of Charles Chauncey, Hugh Peters, and John Winthrop—Winthrop, however, not taking a degree.

Oxford, at the same time, was credited with about a score of matriculants who finally came to New England. But the list fails to contain names so outstanding as the Cambridge registers offer. About a third of the names belong to Mag-

[1] For these facts I am indebted to a most weighty and informing tract, *The Influence of the English Universities in the Development of New England*, by Franklin B. Dexter, Professor in Yale University. Professor Dexter's paper was originally read, February 12, 1880, before the Massachusetts Historical Society.

dalen and to Magdalen Hall. Christ Church, New College, Queen's, Wadham, and All Souls are credited with one name each.

The reason of the contrast between seventy matriculants of Cambridge and only twenty of Oxford is not far to seek. Cambridge, and especially Emmanuel, was a Puritan seed-plot, and this plot received an ecclesiastical and even a clerical cultivation. Sir Walter Mildmay, who founded the College in 1584, said in his nineteenth statute he desired it to be known that the study of theology was to be made the chief subject in his College, in order to raise up preachers, and not administrators of the sacraments. The Puritanism of Cambridge stands out in deepest contrast to the Tory tenets of Oxford. In the year 1603 the Vice-Chancellor, the Doctors and the Heads of houses of Oxford made answer to a "humble petition" of Puritan ministers of the Church of England desiring reformation of certain ceremonies and abuses of the Church. These ministers had made a petition to the King for ecclesiastical reforms. The answer of Oxford stigmatized the petitioners as "absurd Brownists," as having "a self-conceited confidence," and as holding "pestilent and blasphemous conclusions." Such an academic interpretation would not attract the sons of Puritan families.

The causes of the presence of learned men in the Bay Colony—and their number was as great in proportion to the whole population as could be found in any similar number of people in the world—and the causes of the absence of such men at Plymouth are not far to seek.

The most obvious of the reasons is found in the fact that the Pilgrim Company was of a lowly and humble origin. In his farewell letter John Robinson says that "you are not furnished with any persons of special eminency above the rest." Their employments at Leyden indicate their social condition. They were of the order of weavers, hat-makers, journeymen, masons, and carpenters. A few became known as "merchants." They were not of the classes which furnished matriculants to university registers. In fact, only three of the Pilgrim families can be traced to English homes. The Pilgrims belonged to the great body of the commonality whence have come no small share of the brawn and brain of the English stock.

Be it also said, that the Pilgrims were what is known as Separatists. Their presence at either university, even if they had desired to attend, would not have been allowed, and it is apparent that they did not desire to attend. Being Separatists from the Church of England, they were also Separatists from the English universities. Those, however, who came to Massachusetts Bay were not, on leaving England, Separatists. They were members of the English Church. They came bearing university degrees. Among them were found the great men who ultimately led that colony to noblest achievements in a new civilization.

The primary and the ultimate truth, moreover, seems to be that it was not education as certainly as it was not trade, that it was not government any more than it was "worldly prosperity," which formed the moving impulse in the Pilgrims' bosom. The fact is that RELIGION was that impulse and motive. The history of the Separatists in England in the closing years of the sixteenth and the first years of the seventeenth century makes plain the fact that the Christian faith as they interpreted it was to them more than life. For this faith they suffered manifold persecutions. They were deprived of their property; they were cast into prison; and for it six of them died. The martyrs were: Dennis, Copping, Thacker, Barrowe, Greenwood, and Penry. In allegiance to their faith they moved to Holland. The annals of the Church at Leyden also give proof of a similar and deepest religious conviction. They endured residence in Holland—though the citizens gave them ample opportunities in freedom of living and of work—"as seeing Him who is invisible." Their preparation for emigration to the New World offers similar evidence of the fundamental character of their religious convictions and constitution. They emigrated as a Church, or as a part of a Church, containing the "youngest and strongest members." Their farewell was a Church farewell; their good-byes were ecclesiastical benedictions. Robinson's farewell letter is filled with invocations and prayers for divine blessings to rest upon them. Of the four reasons which Bradford in his immortal History gives for the emigration, the last is by far the most important:—

"Lastly, (and which was not least,) a great hope & inward zeall they had of laying some good foundation, or at least to make some way thereunto, for ye propagating & advancing ye gospell of ye kingdom of Christ in those remote parts of ye world; yea, though they should be but even as stepping-stones unto others for ye performing of so great a work."[2]

The life of the Pilgrims, once arrived in Plymouth, was also the religious life. Lacking certain of the specifically religious requirements laid down by the citizens of the Bay Colony, it was yet in atmosphere and influence, in belief and practice, in family and individual, in principle and application, in purpose, programme, and achievement, religious. Defining religion as primarily an interpretation of the relation which man holds to God, the Pilgrim believed that this relation was constant, intimate, all-pervasive, and all-important. The Pilgrim was not God-intoxicated, like Spinoza; he was rather God-fearing, like Jonathan Edwards. His was not the rationalist's system, which found a God at the end of a syllogism. His point of view was not intellectual. It was rather that of a servant of the Lord of Hosts, willing to be damned for the glory

[2] *History of Plymouth Plantation,* by William Bradford (the second Governor of the Colony), p. 24.

of his Creator, Preserver, and bountiful Benefactor. His possessions, though he gained them by a racial energy and held them by a racial prudence and sagacity, represented a trusteeship which he sought to fulfill well. His Master's name was on his forehead; and his Master's sake was his abiding motive. Prayer was to him not a vain petition, but an act of faith which could move mountains. He was, here and now, a citizen of God's kingdom.

Bradford's precious History is filled with incidents and allusions which prove and illustrate the primary religious character of the little settlement. As its members were in trouble and in danger, seeking their way to the shelter of an unknown harbor, they found a gift of God in "a *morning* of comforte & refreshing (as usually he doth to his children)."[3] When sickness was afflicting others the Lord upheld them, so that "they were not at all infected either with sicknes, or lamnes."[4] When famine was upon them and "begane now to pinch them sore, they not knowing what to doe, the Lord, (who never fails his,) presents them with an occasion, beyond all expectation."[5] It was declared, too, that "it hath plased God to stirre up ye harts of our adventurers"[6] to give them sorely needed aid. Upon another occasion it was plain that "the eminente

[3] *Ibid.*, p. 87.
[4] *Ibid.*, p. 91.
[5] *Ibid.*, p. 124.
[6] *Ibid.*, p. 158.

hand of God to be with them, and his blesing upon them."[7] The Pilgrim did not write of the immanence of God; but the indwelling of God in his spirit and the presence of God in his environment was to him vital, constant, comprehensive, fundamental, inspiring, and directive.

Religion may exist without the Bible, but the Christian religion which the Pilgrims possessed and which possessed them is a religion founded on the Bible. They received the book as their ecclesiastical creed and as a sailing-chart for the voyage of each day and of every year. Its Ten Commandments were to be obeyed implicity and explicitly. Its Levitical laws were to be observed, and the penalties of the violation of these laws were to be, and were, applied. The application of these laws in capital punishment, a punishment which was recognized as befitting as many as eight crimes, was strictly observed.

The Christian religion is founded not only upon a belief in God and on the Bible as a revelation of His will and mind, but also on the derivation from the Bible of the observance of the Sabbath as a day of rest in the field and the home, and as a day of worship in the "meeting-house." But far more important than the observance of the Sabbath as a part of the Biblical and Christian economy was the doctrine of the Church. The Church, according to the Pilgrim conception, was fundamental to the individual and to society.

[7] *Ibid.*, p. 172.

That doctrine taught that a church was a complete entity or unity in itself. It was a body segregated from constitutional or vital relationships with other bodies or churches. It had complete power unto, and in, and of, itself. It was not governed by bishops, it was not controlled by an oligarchy; it was a democracy, sufficient for its own existence, present and future. It was, in and of itself, an individual divine and human corporation. When coming to hold relationships to similar bodies, it would have been called, in modern phrase, a Congregational church in the United States, or an Independent one in England. But in the Mayflower time the Pilgrim Church was an individual religious unit. Such a unit incarnated and illustrated the religious belief and practice of the Pilgrim Company.

After two generations the Plymouth Colony ceased to exist as a civil and political unit and agency. Its fortunes became joined with the interests of the more prosperous Bay Colony, of richer soil, of deeper harbors, of greater numbers, and of nobler intellectual interests. But while it lasted as a distinct unit it stood for the power of religion. The Bay Colony also stood for the power and place of religion, of education too, and of other great civil and personal elements as well. Henceforth the two settlements, Pilgrim and Puritan, were to be united.

For two and a half centuries and more these two bodies have formed, and still continue to form, a river of influence which has served and has determined American life to a degree greater than any historical prophet or prophetic historian would have dared to predict. From the twenty-one thousand persons who came to New England between 1620 and 1640, when emigration in large numbers ceased—because of the calling of the Long Parliament,—have sprung, directly or indirectly, not far from four million persons. In the four million, at least a strain of English blood may be found. From this number also have come forth great personalities which have largely dominated American life, made American achievement, inspired American thought, and formed national character. Of course there are outstanding exceptions. George Washington of Virginia is one whose immigrant ancestor came to Virginia. Abraham Lincoln of Kentucky is only an apparent exception, for his immigrant ancestor settled in Hingham of Massachusetts. But in general this number of twenty-one thousand persons, or four thousand families, have given birth and being to the men and women who have served to keep and to transmit the Anglo-Saxon ideals of the commonwealth, of the family, of liberty supported by law, of law inspired by liberty, of pure morality, of the worth of the individual, of education, and of religion, as the regnant forces in American life and character.

As I close this chapter, I desire to call attention to one, and to only one, inference among the many which might be drawn from this survey. It is the inference that religion separated from education is in peril of becoming narrow, inhuman, dogmatic, severe in tone, reactionary in statement and act, uninteresting, self-destructive. It nurtures man as a citizen of one world only, and that not chiefly the present. It builds the church; it erects the altar; it reads the Holy Scriptures. It does not build the all-comprehensive and eternal city of God. Education without religion, it may be added, also becomes narrow, tends to become technical, over-intellectual, over-individualistic, unsympathetic, radical, lacking highest motives, materialistic. Education alone and unaided interprets man as a citizen of one world only, and that not of the world to which religion inspires and points him. The Pilgrims' motive, nobly religious and ecclesiastical in its origin and staying power, was obliged to unite itself, though unconsciously to itself, with the intellectual, educated, and educating forces of its neighboring Colony. It thus not only saved itself, but also helped to save New England and the new world beyond the western seas in the successive generations.

IV

THE EFFECT OF THE EUROPEAN WAR ON HIGHER LEARNING IN AMERICAN SOCIETY [*]

The effect of the war upon the higher learning of America is as nothing compared to its effect on the higher learning of the nations at war. Neither the number of students nor the annual income has been affected in an appreciable degree. A few American professors have found their sabbatical vacations interrupted, and a few hundreds of students who had proposed to go to Germany or France or England for graduate or other work have been obliged to change their plans. German books and periodicals come not at all to the libraries, or come irregularly. Pieces of physical and chemical apparatus, made best and cheapest in Germany, are not to be bought. Certain fields of research in these and other sciences are not cultivated by reason of the lack of proper tools. But beyond these and other similar resulting conditions, the war brings no special suffering to the normal course of the more material part of our higher education.

[*] October, 1915.

Although the interest, too, of American teachers and students in the Great War is not at all comparable with the interest of their European brothers, yet this interest cuts down deep into the heart and mind. The movements of the campaigns are followed, the victories and the defeats quicken or depress, the value of the forces is estimated, and the prognosis is debated. The sympathy of at least nineteen-twentieths of all academic people is with the Allies. The most common remark made about Germany is that she is obsessed. The feeling toward her is rather one of pity than of anger, and rather one of emotional anger than of hatred. That the final triumph will represent a victory for the Allies is not deeply doubted, but that the war will be a long one is generally conceded in academic companies.

It is also to be said that at least five medical schools with affiliated hospitals have sent delegations from their instructing and hospital staffs to the field. The Western Reserve University Medical School and its affiliated Lakeside Hospital was the first to send a unit of twelve representatives, having for its head Dr. George W. Crile. Already Harvard has followed with a second unit, and other schools are to succeed. These services represent a contribution which the university medical schools are glad to offer.

The effects of the war on the studies of teachers and students form a more complex question, as it is a more general one. The effects differ according to the character of the studies themselves. For instance, the effect upon the pursuit of the ancient classics in American colleges could on the whole be neglected. My associates say that apparently the subjects of their teaching in Latin and Greek do not suffer even a temporary loss. But outside of these fields, permanent results are to be seen in most of the departments established in American universities and colleges. For instance, a distinguished teacher of biology writes:

"It is evident that the biological value of the war diminishes rapidly with the perfection of military weapons and machinery, all tending to an indiscriminate slaughter more and more complete. The element of personal encounter and the matching of individual brawn, wit, or prowess is more and more reduced, to the present moment, when they must be regarded as negative quantities. Though it requires the highest degree of skill to design modern weapons, but little is needed to use them, and unskilled laborers are marched to the front by thousands in every modern war.

"The present great war is resulting in an indiscriminate eliminating of the fittest physically of all the contending nations, and from the standpoint of eugenics is the greatest calamity that could happen.

"The conquered nations in the present war will undoubtedly in time renew their depleted life, though bled to the last ounce of blood, for statistics seem to prove that in a virile race hard conditions tend to increase the percentage of male births, and to stimulate variation; by thus favoring adaptation, the race may be tided over a period of crisis, however acute. The decision of the present war will depend upon other facts than biological fitness, and the result can be nothing less than a colossal biological waste.

"As a partial balance to the overwhelming tide of baser passions engendered by every war, whether of victor or vanquished, we have to recognize the *esprit de corps* and communism which are usually developed, and which may be regarded in the light of victory though bought at a wholly ruinous price."

The results which will be wrought in the subjects of modern languages are, of course, also great and diverse. Perhaps the effect upon the teaching of the German language will be the most marked. One of my colleagues, a professor of German, says:

"It is my opinion (expressed, however, with the diffidence that becomes a prophet) that the position of German as a subject for teaching and for research will not be altered if Germany is unsuccessful in the present war. Materialism and militarism have been in a fair way to kill off all that is best in Germany. Defeat should restore the nation to its wholesome self."

Another distinguished teacher of this language says:

"As I see things now, the effect will be hurtful,

chiefly because the sympathy of the American people is not with the Germans in the conflict. Whether rightly or wrongly, the average American holds Germany in a large measure responsible for the war, forgets what that great people has done and been in the past, regards Prussian militarism as the sentiment of the whole nation, and construes natural German patriotism, once war is started, as the expression of a desire to rule the world. Such a feeling, I think, is strong and cannot fail to turn our young people away from German study. Of course, it should do the opposite, for if we cannot agree with another, we should study him all the harder, in order to understand him better; but I fear it will not be so in this case.

"If Germany should win in the war, I think this lack of sympathy would change into a still stronger feeling, which would only make matters worse. If she should lose, I fear her loss of prestige would still further lessen American interest. And whether she win or lose, she herself will be set back half a century in all the arts of peace: to my mind, the best claim any people can make to the interest of another."

The intimations of what the effect of the conflict will be upon the French language and literature give promise that the results will be still more marked and impressive than upon the Teutonic. One professor of literature speaks of the French conditions as follows:

"An editor of a leading firm of publishers of

college and high-school text-books wrote me last September that he foresaw a considerable increase in the number of students of French owing to the European war. I am unable to say on what grounds his prediction is based, but it has been realized at least in our College. Reports from two important universities further west indicate a similar state of affairs. The cause, or one of the causes, may be a reaction of the evident sympathy of the American public with the side of the Allies. After the war increased travel will probably be indulged in by Americans, who will want to visit places and countries made memorable by great events. To this effect a conversational knowledge of French will be an almost indispensable adjunct, and such a knowledge will be rightly desired by students who contemplate going abroad. We shall have to meet such a demand in a manner that will not interfere harmfully with the study of the literary masterpieces.

"As far as research studies are concerned, it is a well-known fact that since the French universities have offered foreigners the same opportunities and prerogatives that their own youth enjoys, Americans whose elders used to go to Germany even for advanced work in Romance tongues, have turned to France in yearly increasing numbers. The war is likely to accentuate this movement, because of the enhanced prestige France will derive from her eventual victory, or through a realization that Germany may lose her position as a great world-power. The experience of the present struggle must also bring home to thinking people the fact that German culture, which started from a highly idealistic basis, has somewhat deteriorated in the keeping of her modern representatives.''

The effect of the war on the whole domain of philosophy it would be extremely difficult to prophesy. One finds it hard to accept the fact that the nation of Kant has so far forgotten herself as to be at war with the lands in which the influence of Kant has been so mighty. It is to be noted, however, that a follower of Kant, Fichte, has in his idealistic and egoistic philosophy laid a very deep and almost forgotten cause of the present obsession. It also seems to me not improbable that the great conception of Schopenhauer, in presenting the world as will, has had a formative and evilly inspiring force far greater than is commonly recognized in either England or the United States. For, as Schopenhauer declares, 'The Will has all of the excellences and none of the defects of the Intellect. It is the original, essential, and primary element of existence; the Intellect is the derived, the accidental, the secondary.' ''[1]

---

[1] The following, gathered up from Schopenhauer's principal work, *Die Welt als Wille und Vorstellung*, is a summary of the excellences of the Will and of the defects of the Intellect:

''The Intellect flags; the Will is unwearied. . . . All cognition is connected with exertion; but Willing is the essence of our being, whose manifestations continue without trouble and of themselves. . . . Will alone is uninvited; often, therefore, it is

But, aside from the interpretations of Schopenhauer, there are many sides of our philosophy which are touched by the great conflict. One of my colleagues writes with wit and sadness:

"The war supplies no end of material for the illustration of principles in psychology and ethics, and they keep crowding upon me in the classroom, though of course I try to avoid using them. Treitschke, Bernhardi, *et al.*, with their outspoken defense of strong-arm methods to win a place in the sun, do not seem to me so very different from any other revolutionists who feel that the rules of the game were made for the benefit of someone else at their expense. England's past 'thefts' and present 'hypocrisy,' as described by those amiable Germans, are quite comparable to the

too ready and too strong in its activity. . . . From the lack of weariness of the Will arises the fault which is more or less common to all men, and which can only be overcome by education. . . . Scarcely have we seized and hastily connected by cognition a few data regarding the circumstances in question . . . than out of the depths of our being arises, uninvited, the ever-ready, never-tiring Will, and manifests itself as terror, fear, hope, pleasure, desire, envy, sorrow, zeal, anger, courage. . . . The Intellect is to the Will in man what the bridle and bit is to the unbroken horse: it must be led by the bridle, it must be instructed or educated, or it is as wild and fierce as the power shown in the dashing waterfall. . . .'

"Will is the essence not only of man, but of the world. 'The world itself is an enormous Will constantly rushing into life.' It manifests itself not only in the desire and struggle of man to live, but also in the conservation of all natural forces: in gravitation . . . in chemical activity, in perdurability and inflexibility, in electricity and magnetism, and in the alternating growth and decay of vegetable life. . . . At all times and in all places the Will strives for a manifestation of itself; nowhere does it find a limit, any complete gratification, any point of rest." It is at this stage of the development of his philosophy that Schopenhauer's theory of pessimism appears.

past and present sins of landed proprietors, mine-holders, and the idle rich. In each case the party in possession of the world's goods invokes an existing moral code for his protection, and in each case the party that envies him demands a revision, and is willing, if need be, to fight for it. In both cases the revolutionists would find much to support them in the ethical conceptions of James and Dewey. Moral code is a matter of will, not of personal principles, declares James in his *Essentials of a Moral Universe,* and Dewey is never tired of declaring that the rules of morality must change continually to meet new conditions, and thus help realize man's ultimate end—abundance of life. And yet I am against the Germans! Thus you see that from the standpoint of ethics the war arouses the most vital of all problems.

"As to the broader and more abstract phases of philosophy, when you find a man like Eucken joining with Haeckel in the cheap pamphleteering they have indulged in, with all its bias and calumny, it is easy to realize that belligerent philosophers can teach us very much more about mob psychology than about the things of the spirit.

"As to the philosophy of religion, the war simply illustrates and accents the need for a pretty radical revision, or rather a thorough reconsideration, of traditional conceptions, in the spirit of democratic generosity. The Kaiser's impious exclusive partnership with God finds its parallel in Psalms that we read religiously in divine service, and while we raise our thanksgiving hymns of praise to the Providence that gave us peace and plenty, it is hard to keep from wondering what some poor Belgian thinks of Providence whose pregnant wife is murdered and whose daughter is outraged before his eyes. Vested interests in theology do not count for much more than vested interests in empire at a time like this."

Another philosopher says:

"One cannot but be struck by the phenomenon of the leading lights in German philosophy uniting so wholeheartedly in the active moral support of the German military cause, but all that it seems legitimately to infer from this is that philosophic calm and the breadth of vision which should characterize the contemplations of the philosopher are ideals which quite lose their power when the primitive instincts of man or the patriotic prejudices of a nation are aroused." [2]

But this war of the world has its most fundamental relations with the sciences that are called social. The war belongs to society,—to humanity.

[3] As I was making the final revision of this manuscript, I found a sketch, written by Professor George Herbert Palmer of Harvard, of his colleague, Josiah Royce. Royce, one of the greatest of American philosophers, was a student of Kant and of Kant's followers. Professor Palmer says of him, "His belief in the crimes of Germany, the land of his spiritual birth, pursued him day and night and had considerable influence in bringing about his death. When the quiet scholar stepped on the public platform to speak of the war, his moral passion swayed the entire audience and much of the world outside." (Quoted from *The Development of Harvard University, Since the Inauguration of President Eliot 1869-1929.* Edited by Samuel Eliot Morison, p. 14.)

It is the conflict of men. It belongs to governments, which are composed of men. It belongs to economics, which is the science of man. It belongs to that vast and still forming field of sociology, the science of men in relation to each other as human beings. It belongs to history. In this vast four-square field of political science, economics, history, and sociology the war is having its most tremendous effects. One teacher of government writes:

"As to government in general, the war has raised the issue between modern social democracy, as exemplified in England, and the bureaucratic, militaristic system of Prussianized Germany. The suddenness and irresponsibility with which war was declared is explained by the autocratic nature of the Prussian-German Imperial Government. The German people looked on as spectators, while one man, the Kaiser, by a stroke of his pen, plunged all Europe into conflict.

"After the war, when the nations come to reckon up profit and loss, I think it is not unlikely that safeguards will be thrown about the right to declare war. I look for the German people to insist upon far-reaching changes in the government in the direction of greater responsibility of the Emperor and his ministers to the representatives of the people in Parliament. It seems probable that Russia, if she succeeds with the help of her Allies in treading down Prussian militarism, will receive an infusion of liberalism.

The triumph of democratic England and France and the fate in which Prussianism will be involved, cannot but have an effect upon her. I should not be surprised to see the Russian people advance to a greater measure of self-government.

"Another significant result which this war has already achieved is the complete vindication of the enlightened British colonial policy of the latter half of the nineteenth century. The wisdom of that policy has frequently been questioned even by the Englishmen, who harked back to the eighteenth-century colonial ideas; and the loose tie between England and her colonies has been scoffed at by Germans as a sign of weakness and pending disintegration. Such doubts as these will now have vanished.

"As for International Law, a victory for the Allied Powers would strengthen the respect in which it is held among nations. If Germany can be made to pay dearly for her ruthless violations, the sanction of International Law will become all the more effectual. But, putting aside this assumption of victory for the Allies, there is much evidence that the consciences of the nations at war and of neutral nations are sensitive upon the subject of violations of International Law. All of the belligerents seem animated by a desire to set themselves right in the eyes of neutral nations, and neutral opinion seems to be exercising a perceptible influence in restraining further possible violations. My opinion is that International Law will emerge from the war with undiminished prestige.

"When the horrors of this war are fully known, there will be a revulsion of sentiment in favor of the humane regulations contained in the Hague Conferences. Undoubtedly at a future Hague Convention certain practices of the present war will be the objects of prohibitory legislative action.

"In respect of maritime warfare, the present war has already brought some backward steps. England has been disposed, so great is her desire to cut off Germany commercially, to push her belligerent rights somewhat beyond the terms of the London Declaration in dealing with neutral commerce. Whether in future England can be led to consent to an enlarged freedom of private property at sea in war time is somewhat problematical.

"I anticipate that the war will stimulate an interest in the study of International Law and Diplomacy. The American public has been acquiring knowledge of the recent history of Europe at a rapid rate, but the subject of International Law is not yet popularized."

A teacher of sociology writes:

"As to the effect of the war on sociology both as a subject for teaching and for research, I suggest that on the whole it will be auspicious, especially in America. Among the warring nations, the evil will largely outweigh the good for at least a generation to come. This will be more apparent if we analyze the conceivable efforts of the conflict into their good and bad components:

"1. The war has stimulated and will stimulate a tremendous amount of interest in social relations generally, and in the causes and the effects of the war as a social phenomenon particularly, a good and useful result. America has long been the scene of intense interest in social questions. Contrast Germany, where to this day there is not a single chair of sociology. This does not mean that social problems do not occupy the Germans, but it does mean that Americans were among the first to believe in the possibility of a science of society and that ascertainable social laws have a practical bearing. To the further development of sociology in the United States, therefore, the present war will give a powerful impetus. More departments of sociology will be established, and more students and teachers.

"2. On the other hand, it will revive a number of biases which make blind to facts and cloud judgment—an unmitigated evil, hurtful in the pursuit of many sciences, but especially fatal in sociological research.

"If we examine the facts underlying the second proposition, we find that no science has suffered as has the science of society from various biases present in the minds of its votaries. We can observe the operations of the religious bias and the class bias, but chief among all the patriotic bias. How this bias works out is well illustrated in the present war in the wholesale renunciation of foreign honors and degrees—from the point of view of the neutral, an extremely puerile display of national vanity. When we realize the importance of comparative methods for the student of human institutions, we begin to see what havoc with judgment and the results of research the injection of such puerile and childish sentiments and prejudices will wreak. The biologist or the engineer has no such difficulties to contend with. A French scientist accepts without misgiving the statement of a German that a certain insect has parasitic habits, for he knows the German has no motive to misinterpret the facts. If a German sociologist, however, affirms that the French people are 'degenerate' or their 'institutions inferior,' there is trouble at once. National pride is aroused. For the sociologist the human group is what the bug is to the biologist. But he approaches the object of his study not with the dispassionate, scientific interest of the latter, but with an ethnocentric or national prejudice which leads him to cherish and overvalue the characteristics of his own group at the expense of foreign or outgroups. This attitude is akin to that of the missionary who is shocked by the religious customs and beliefs of those whom he has come to convert. It is the human equation, which in sciences like physics and biology is negligible. It has always been the bane of sociology. Now, whatever tends to increase this basis, as war does, is inimical to the scientific spirit of sociology. This state of affairs bodes a dark day for the social sciences of Europe.

"As for sociological research, the results cannot but be beneficent. In the first place, the war should serve to dispel several illusions as to the character of human society, and lead to a greater measure of agreement among sociologists. Such questions as whether society is 'subjective' or an 'objective' reality must be discarded as metaphysics. Likewise the problem of a progress must be given up. If the present war has demonstrated anything, it has shown that there is a tragical sameness about all human events. What Lyell asserted of geological evolution is equally true of human society. The forces in operation today must be conceived to have operated during all past time; *i.e.*, as far as human society is concerned, its character, as determined by the nature of man and by the life conditions on the earth, has remained the same from primitive times to the present. Nothing sets forth the fundamental needs and interests of socictics as does war. Those interests, for the warring nations, have narrowed down to two: food and men. The commissariat and population policies, as expressed in the reported suspension of marriage bans in Austria and of marriage fees in England—how significant are these facts! How primitive the motives back of them!

"The war is bound to have a sobering effect

upon students of society. The search for panaceas and Utopias, as well as the eugenic dream of a 'superman,' should be given up. If the social scientists can learn to deal with men as they are and with conditions as they are, there is hope that sociology will grow into a science valid in theory and practical in bearings. The war should give an impulse in that direction. By freeing the subject of accessories and side-issues, it should have the effect of making research more purposeful and more truly utilitarian. This is all to the good of the American student who makes even the slightest attempt at maintaining his 'mental neutrality' and cultivating a spirit of scientific fairness and impartiality. Sociology has a bright future in our country."

Upon economics the effect of the war will be still more marked. A professor of that great subject writes:

"Much has been made of the economic explanation of the struggle. For example, the alleged importance to Germany of colonial outlets for her manufactures and emigration. Doubtless there will be a reconsideration of the relative significance of economic factors as compared with other influences, such as the spirit of nationality, upon the situation that led up to the conflagration. A clearer understanding of these forces may result in a truer evaluation of their importance and a more rational reaction of the human spirit subject to their influence. Pleas like Norman Angell's may have a readier hearing and more effective influence upon public policy.

"If the reaction after the war turns the minds of men toward the peaceable fruit of social righteousness, there will be a strong interest in the study of economics for an understanding of the material reconstruction of shattered human relationships. The previous equilibrium among labor, capital, and natural resources will have been disturbed, and a readjustment will have to be sought that will distribute the results of production among them in somewhat different proportions, thus affecting rates of real wages, interest, and economic rents. While nothing so revolutionary is to be anticipated as the effect of the Black Death in 1348, which depleted the labor supply and radically altered the economic status of the laborers and methods of agriculture, still the great destruction of life now going on is bound to be felt economically. It is true that the reduction of the supply of labor has been accompanied by devastation and vast expenditure of wealth that might have been used as capital, but it is improbable that the two types of losses have been in the same degree. It is probable that we underestimate the recuperative powers of society in recovery from losses of property. Forced economy that would lead to a stoppage of waste would rapidly replace the material values destroyed. Nevertheless considerable adjustment, demanding an appreciable length of time, will be necessary to meet the new proportion in which the factors in production will occur. From this task of finding a new equilibrium will arise problems both in research and exposition that will test the powers of observation and reasoning.

"Whether we turn to the fundamental forces that govern human conduct, or to the field of public policy relating to international trade, or to the distribution of wealth among the producers, the outcome of the war, assuming that it will continue at the present rate of destruction over a period of years, is bound to have an epoch-making influence on the economic interest of mankind and hence upon the science concerned with these interests. To predict in detail would require the prescience of a seer. These broad generalities, I fear, will not be of much interest. I can only plead that a prophet's real function is not to foretell but to lead to repentance."

I now come to a brief statement of the effect of the war upon history. For, as I have intimated, the war is the result and the cause of tremendous historical movements. If one could hint what Europe will be, after the signing of certain treaties, he would indeed be a prophet. But if one wisely decline to figure in such a rôle, one can refer to such minor effects upon ourselves as students and teachers of history. Two teachers of the great subject whom I have consulted believe that the war is greatly stimulating the study of the subject. Teachers will offer more courses in the recent history of Europe. It also will open up a field of tremendous importance for research. The current discussions of the origin of the war, the division of responsibility, and the evidence of atrocities will in the not remote future come under the microscopic and telescopic eye of investigation. One teacher adds:

"It seems to me that the history teacher, on the defensive for his subject before a world too little appreciative of historical values, finds his position suddenly strengthened; for the war brings into strong relief his contention that only a knowledge and understanding of the past can make the present intelligible."

This compilation of interpretations and of judgments, which might be greatly prolonged, illustrates several great truths.

It illustrates the intimacy of the ties binding nation to nation. These ties are not simply diplomatic understandings and political alliances. They are also deep relationships covering every part of the life of man. No nation can say to another nation, "I have no need of thee." The relations are the growth of generations of struggle and of mingled fellowship and enmity. Any breaking of these ties throws each of these relationships out of its proper place. Education among them is thus made to suffer. Its place in the sun is obscured, its laws are broken, and its workings interrupted.

This review also illustrates the duty of the educationalist to make use of this war to enforce certain great truths which times of peace cannot enforce. Among these truths are the worth of history as a subject to study, the importance of international law, the significance of the different types of nationalities, the advantages and disadvantages of different forms of political government, and, most timely of all, the effect of the devastation wrought by war on the highest life of the nations.

This review also enforces the lessons that nations, as well as individuals, should stand for the noblest type of being. It furthermore illustrates the duty of each nation to stand for a noble type of individual life and of international conduct and relations. One would like to believe that the war would promote such understanding as now consciously or unconsciously controls the bearing of individual men toward each other. That great word "Gentleman" I should like to enlarge into the word "Gentlestate." The Gentlestate should exist for all of its citizens, and all of its citizens should exist for it. Reciprocity of rights and duties should be the rule. The Gentlestate may be the center and source of power, but, if it possess the giant's strength, it is too great to use it like a giant. It seeks to do justice, to love mercy, and it walks humbly. If it has enemies, it treats them as if they were to become its friends. It has too much good sense to be responsive to insults and too much generosity to bear malice. It is too eager about great things to be annoyed by small irritations, and too much concerned about the good of all to be keen about any lack of respect to itself. It seeks to see the large as large, the small as small, the ephemeral as of the day, and the lasting as permanent, being ever guided by a sense of proportion. It respects the rights of other states with that same honesty and integrity which it merits from others. It makes few or no demands. It has no occasion for self-defense. It seeks only to have deserts. It is tolerant of others' weaknesses, patient toward their limitations, never finding in either weakness or limitation any excuse for its own aggrandizement. It seeks to enrich as well as to be enriched, to enlarge as well as to be enlarged, and it vastly prefers rather to be the victim than the agent of any misinterpretation or wrong-doing. Its protective policy is to shield the weak, and its free-trade theory is to give every other state more than it demands. This Gentlestate is considerate in thought and feeling, without either hardness or mysticism, cordial without effusiveness, forceful and direct without harshness, firm in conviction without obstinacy, of the highest idealism, ever exercising a goodwill without giving any impression of weakness. This Gentlestate has no armies and no battleships for attacking on either land or sea. Its chief fortresses are the cardinal virtues and the cardinal graces of faith and hope for humanity's future and of love for humanity itself.

V

THE AMERICAN CIVIL WAR AND THE GREAT WAR: A COMPARISON *

Love of liberty and love of country are the dominating and inspiring aims of most wars. The Civil War in the United States of America embodied these two great human and national principles. The two principles, however, were the objects of different interpretations and applications, as made by the belligerent powers. The Confederate States believed it was their right, under both the fundamental law of liberty and the written law of the Constitution, to withdraw from the Union. This right they saw fit to exercise for what seemed to them sufficient reason. In order actually to secure certain results, made possible they believed by their secession, they fought. These results were partly and only partly summed up in the word "slavery." As the war proceeded from year to year they believed that they were fighting not simply to protect the institution of slavery, but also to defend the integrity of each of their own Confederated States. The war was for them a war *pro aris et focis,* in both an economic system and a political interpretation.

* October, 1916.

The Federal States also fought the war under the power of the same great principles of liberty and of patriotism, with a fundamental difference in interpretation. It was a war for the Union, for the preservation of the nation as one and undivided; and it was also a war for the abolition of negro slavery. These two fundamental principles were at the beginning of the contest more or less united in the thinking of the North, and they became more united as the contest proceeded. Yet be it said that at the beginning of the contest there were those who declared that the conflict was a conflict purely for or against the Union: slavery did not form, they affirmed, a constitutional element in the question. There was also a party to whom the constitutional relation seemed insignificant—who emphasized the controlling part or function which slavery had played and was apparently destined to play in the struggle.

Upon this central and duplex problem the testimony of Lincoln has supreme value, as it has upon other elements of the American conflict.

In notes for speeches made in 1858, Lincoln wrote:

"I believe the government cannot endure permanently half slave and half free. I expressed this belief a year ago; and subsequent developments have but confirmed me. I do not expect the Union to be dissolved. I do not expect the house to fall; but I do expect it will cease to be divided. It will become all one thing or all the other. Either the opponents of slavery will arrest the further spread of it, and put it in course of ultimate extinction; or its advocates will push it forward till it shall become alike lawful in all the States, old as well as new."[1]

He also said:

"Welcome or unwelcome, agreeable or disagreeable, whether this shall be an entire slave nation is the issue before us. Every incident—every little shifting of scenes or of actors—only clears away the intervening trash, compacts and consolidates the opposing hosts, and brings them more and more distinctly face to face. The conflict will be a severe one; and it will be fought through by those who do care for the result, and not by those who do not care—by those who are for, and those who are against, a legalized national slavery."[2]

He also said, in an address given in New York City, 20th February, 1861, a few days before he took office:

"This Union shall never be abandoned, unless the possibility of its existence shall cease to exist without the necessity of throwing passengers and cargo overboard. So long, then, as it is possible that the prosperity and liberties of this people can be preserved within this Union, it shall be my purpose at all times to preserve it."[3]

Again, near the same date, to the Senate of New Jersey he spoke:

[1] *Complete Works*, Vol. IV, p. 233.
[2] *Ibid.*, Vol. IV, p. 235.
[3] *Ibid.*, Vol. VI, p. 150.

"I am exceedingly anxious that this Union, the Constitution, and the liberties of the people shall be perpetuated in accordance with the original idea for which that struggle was made, and I shall be most happy indeed if I shall be a humble instrument in the hands of the Almighty and of this, his almost chosen people, for perpetuating the object of that great struggle." [4]

In a letter to Horace Greeley, 22nd August, 1862, Lincoln wrote:

"I would save the Union. I would save it the shortest way under the Constitution. The sooner the national authority can be restored, the nearer the Union will be 'the Union as it was.' If there be those who would not save the Union unless they could at the same time save slavery, I do not agree with them. If there be those who would not save the Union unless they could at the same time destroy slavery, I do not agree with them. My paramount object in this struggle is to save the Union, and is not either to save or to destroy slavery. If I could save the Union without freeing any slave, I would do it; and if I could save it by freeing all the slaves, I would do it; and if I could save it by freeing some and leaving others alone, I would also do that. What I do about slavery and the colored race, I do because I believe it helps to save the Union; and what I forbear, I forbear because I do not believe it would help to save the Union. I shall do less whenever

[4] *Ibid.*, Vol. VI, pp. 151-2.

I shall believe what I am doing hurts the cause, and I shall do more whenever I shall believe doing more will help the cause."[5]

In his Annual Message to Congress, 1st December, 1862, he declared:

"Among the friends of the Union there is great diversity of sentiment and of policy in regard to slavery and the African race amongst us. Some would perpetuate slavery; some would abolish it suddenly and without compensation; some would abolish it gradually, and with compensation; some would remove the freed people from us, and some would retain them with us; and there are yet other minor diversities. Because of these diversities we waste much strength in struggles among ourselves. By mutual concession we should harmonize and act together. This would be compromise; but it would be compromise among the friends, and not with the enemies, of the Union."[6]

These quotations, the number and fullness of which could be greatly increased, are sufficient to prove: (1) that the American Civil War was, on the side of the North, fought for the nation's integrity, and, on the side of the South, fought for the right to secede from the Union; and (2) that the cause or reason for certain states wishing to secede from the Union lay in the desire to extend slavery into territory which had hitherto been free from it. Behind the Union cause came to

[5] *Complete Works*, Vol. VIII, pp. 15-16.
[6] *Ibid.*, Vol. VIII, p. 118.

stand the emancipation of the slave; behind the Secession cause stood at the very beginning the perpetuation and the enlargement of slavery. The preservation of the Federal Government might be called the final cause of the war, and the extension of slavery its exciting or creative cause. Comprehensive in judgment, and warming to the heart, Lincoln said as late as the year 1864, in a published interview:

"There have been men base enough to propose to me to return to slavery the black warriors of Port Hudson and Olustee, and thus win the respect of the masters they fought. Should I do so, I should deserve to be damned in time and eternity. Come what will, I will keep my faith with friend and foe. My enemies pretend I am now carrying on this war for the sole purpose of abolition. So long as I am President, it shall be carried on for the sole purpose of restoring the Union. But no human power can subdue this rebellion without the use of the emancipation policy, and every other policy calculated to weaken the moral and physical forces of the rebellion.

"Freedom has given us 150,000 men, raised on Southern soil. It will give us more yet. Just so much it has subtracted from the enemy, and, instead of alienating the South, there are now evidences of a fraternal feeling growing up between our men and the rank and file of the rebel soldiers. Let my enemies prove to the country that the destruction of slavery is not necessary to a restoration of the Union. I will abide the issue."[7]

Again he said, in an address to the 164th Ohio Regiment:

"We have, as all will agree, a free government, where every man has a right to be equal with every other man. In this great struggle, this form of government and every form of human right is endangered if our enemies succeed. There is more involved in this contest than is realized by every one. There is involved in this struggle the question whether your children and my children shall enjoy the privileges we have enjoyed."[8]

To another regiment he spoke:

"It is in order that each one of you may have, through this free government which we have enjoyed, an open field and a fair chance for your industry, enterprise, and intelligence; that you may all have equal privileges in the race of life, with all its desirable human aspirations. It is for this the struggle should be maintained, that we may not lose our birthright—not only for one, but for two or three years. The nation is worth fighting for, to secure such an inestimable jewel."[9]

Like the American Civil War, the present Great War is a contest for liberty and for patriotism. Every nation involved declares, as did the two divisions of the American Commonwealth, that it is contending for either or for both of these fun-

[7] *Complete Works*, Vol. X, p. 191.   [9] *Ibid.*, Vol. X, p. 203.
[8] *Ibid.*, Vol. X, p. 199.

damental and sublime principles. As in the case of the American Commonwealth, the war is differently interpreted in different nations. England is fighting for liberty as against autocracy. As Lord Bryce wrote me a year and a half ago, England is fighting for the preservation of small nations and for the inviolability of treaties. Hers is a real battle for humanity. France is fighting also in love of liberty and of country. Germany is fighting, as she believes, for the attacked and endangered Fatherland. Russia and Italy are inspired also by the patriotic motive. It is not a little significant that in the parallelism which I am intimating the position of England in the present conflict is most akin to the position of the Federal Government in the American contest. The Federal Government, battling for the freedom of the slave, was also battling for the rights of all men to be free: England, fighting Germany, is fighting for the democratic principle everywhere. The Federal Government, fighting for the Union, was fighting for national integrity against a domestic foe; England, fighting Germany, is fighting for the national integrity of Belgium and of other small peoples, and indeed of large peoples, against foreign enemies. Under new conditions and diverse forms New World history comes to repeat itself in the Old World.

In a second aspect of our parallelism, a similarity exists. It refers to the beginning and the conduct of the two wars. For a generation the

Southern States had been preparing for a separation, by peaceable means if possible, by military measures, if necessary.

Lincoln wrote in June, 1863:

"The insurgents had been preparing for it more than thirty years, while the government had taken no steps to resist them. The former had carefully considered all the means which could be turned to their account. It undoubtedly was a well-pondered reliance with them that in their own unrestricted effort to destroy Union, Constitution and law, all together, the Government would, in great degree, be restrained by the same Constitution and law from arresting their progress. Their sympathizers pervaded all departments of the government and nearly all communities of the people. From this material, under cover of 'liberty of speech,' 'liberty of the press,' and *habeas corpus,* they hoped to keep on foot amongst us a most efficient corps of spies, informers, suppliers and aiders and abettors of their cause in a thousand ways." [10]

How akin are these methods to the methods and means and measures adopted by the Germans, with a varying intensity, for a generation also—methods which now lie uncovered in part, and only in part, to the world! Likewise the lack of preparation of the Northern States for war was quite as complete as the lack of preparation on land of England to meet a world-cataclysm. Neither

[10] *Ibid.,* Vol. VIII, p. 302.

could believe that such a catastrophe was possible: both hoped for better things through and for their brothers.

The financial analogy also emerges. Lincoln said, in his Message to Congress, 6th December, 1864:

"The receipts during the year, from all sources, upon the basis of warrants signed by the Secretary of the Treasury, including loans and the balance in the Treasury on the first day of July, 1863, were $1,394,796,007.62, and the aggregate disbursements, upon the same basis, were $1,298,-056,101.89, leaving a balance in the treasury, as shown by warrants, of $96,739,905.73. . . .

"The public debt on the first day of July last, as appears by the books of the treasury, amounted to $1,740,690,489.49. Probably, should the war continue for another year, that amount may be increased by not far from $500,000,000. Held as it is, for the most part, by our own people, it has become a substantial branch of national though private property." [11]

It is unnecessary, as it would be impossible, for me to repeat the figures of the cost of the Great War to England and to her Allies. Of course, the amount in both expenditure and income is far in excess of the American figures—as much greater as the number of soldiers and sailors employed in the European conflict is larger than the number engaged in the American. The American Civil

[11] *Ibid.*, Vol. X, pp. 291-2, 293.

War represented the highest cost, in money and men, of any civil war up to the middle of the nineteenth century, as the present war, which is in a sense civil, is the most costly of all wars.

In the ending of the two conflicts, too, is found a likeness of sentiment and of conviction. About nine months before the surrender of General Lee, Lincoln said in June, 1864:

"It is a pertinent question, often asked in the mind privately, and from one to the other, when is the war to end? Surely I feel as deep an interest in this question as any other can; but I do not wish to name a day, a month, or year, when it is to end. I do not wish to run any risk of seeing the time come without our being ready for the end, for fear of disappointment because the time had come and not the end. We accepted this war for an object, a worthy object, and the war will end when that object is attained. Under God, I hope it never will end until that time. Speaking of the present campaign, General Grant is reported to have said, 'I am going through on this line if it takes all summer.' This war has taken three years; it was begun or accepted upon the line of restoring the national authority over the whole national domain, and for the American people, as far as my knowledge enables me to speak, I say we are going through on this line if it takes three years more." [12]

Do not the remarks of Lincoln, speaking more

[12] *Ibid.*, Vol. X, p. 129.

than fifty years ago, and almost a year before the cessation of hostilities, voice the deep feelings of England and of her Allies of the present year and month?

It is also to be noted that after three years of constant fighting the resources of the States of the North were found to be not only unexhausted, but apparently inexhaustible. Lincoln said soon after his second election:

"The election has exhibited another fact, not less valuable to be known—the fact that we do not approach exhaustion in the most important branch of national resources—that of living men. While it is melancholy to reflect that the war has filled so many graves, and carried mourning to so many hearts, it is some relief to know that compared with the surviving, the fallen have been so few. While corps, and divisions, and brigades, and regiments have formed, and fought, and dwindled, and gone out of existence, a great majority of the men who composed them are still living. . . .

We have more men now than we had when the war began; we are not exhausted, nor in process of exhaustion; we are gaining strength, and may, if need be, maintain the contest indefinitely. This as to men. Material resources are now more complete and abundant than ever.

"The national resources, then, are unexhausted, and, as we believe, inexhaustible." [13]

[13] *Ibid.*, Vol. X, pp. 305-6, 307.

England is still unexhausted; and are there not intimations that she is inexhaustible? One of the war songs of the United States ran:

"We are coming, Father Abraham, three hundred thousand strong."

Such in essence is England's soul and voice. Her essential strengths are unimpaired.

Further is it to be said, that in a sense both wars were religious wars. Each side appealed to its God for recognition, guidance, support. Although the German Kaiser has appeared to believe that his partnership with Providence is a bit more legitimate and intimate than that vouchsafed to any other sovereign, yet each nation has seen fit to ask for the special aid of the God of battles. Each ascribes victory as belonging at least in part to the help of divine reënforcements. Protestant, Catholic—of the Catholic faith, both Roman and Greek—and Moslem are alike in the earnestness of their petitions and in the sincerity of their thanksgiving.

The American conflict was likewise religious. On the whole, perhaps the religious element was somewhat more manifest in the South than in the North. But in the North, with which we are now specially concerned, it was also significant. In Lincoln both the religious feeling and the religious belief were dominant. His expressions of religious hope and trust were touched by a deep sense of reverence and of humility, which, it may be added, is in happy contrast to the pious presumptuousness of the German Emperor. From many speeches, letters, and formal papers quotations might be made.

In 1862, in a private note, Lincoln wrote:

"The will of God prevails. In great contests each party claims to act in accordance with the will of God. Both may be, and one must be, wrong. God cannot be for and against the same thing at the same time. In the present civil war it is quite possible that God's purpose is something different from the purpose of either party; and yet the human instrumentalities, working just as they do, are of the best adaptation to effect his purpose. I am almost ready to say that this is probably true; that God wills this contest, and wills that it shall not end yet. By his mere great power on the minds of the now contestants, he could have either saved or destroyed the Union without a human contest. Yet the contest began. And, having begun, he could give the final victory to either side any day. Yet the contest proceeds."[14]

In a letter to Mrs. Gurney he said:

"In the very responsible position in which I happen to be placed, being a humble instrument in the hands of our Heavenly Father, as I am, and as we all are, to work out his great purposes, I have desired that all my works and acts may be

[14] *Ibid.*, Vol. VIII, pp. 52-53.

according to his will, and that it might be so, I have sought his aid; but if, after endeavoring to do my best in the light which he affords me, I find my efforts fail, I must believe that for some purpose unknown to me, he wills it otherwise. If I had had my way, this war would never have been commenced. If I had been allowed my way, this war would have been ended before this; but we find it still continues, and we must believe that he permits it for some wise purpose of his own, mysterious and unknown to us; and though with our limited understandings we may not be able to comprehend it, yet we cannot but believe that he who made the world still governs it."[15]

Again he said:

"I hope it will not be irreverent for me to say that if it is probable that God would reveal his will to others on a point so connected with my duty, it might be supposed he would reveal it directly to me; for, unless I am more deceived in myself than I often am, it is my earnest desire to know the will of Providence in this matter. And if I can learn what it is, I will do it."[16]

In January, 1863, he wrote to a friend:

"It is most cheering and encouraging for me to know that in the efforts which I have made and am making for the restoration of a righteous peace

[15] *Ibid.*, Vol. VIII, pp. 50-51.
[16] *Ibid.*, Vol. VIII, p. 29.

to our country, I am upheld and sustained by the good wishes and prayers of God's people. No one is more deeply than myself aware that without His favor our highest wisdom is but as foolishness and that our most strenuous efforts would avail nothing in the shadow of His displeasure. I am conscious of no desire for my country's welfare that is not in consonance with His will, and of no plan upon which we may not ask His blessing. It seems to me that if there be one subject upon which all good men may unitedly agree, it is imploring the gracious favor of the God of Nations upon the struggles our people are making for the preservation of their precious birthright of civil and religious liberty." [17]

A month later he wrote to the Rev. Alexander Reed:

"And whatever shall tend to turn our thoughts from the unreasoning and uncharitable passions, prejudices, and jealousies incident to a great national trouble such as ours, and to fix them upon the vast and long-enduring consequences, for weal or for woe, which are to result from the struggle, and especially to strengthen our reliance on the Supreme Being for the final triumph of the right, cannot but be well for us all." [18]

To a delegation of Evangelical Lutherans, in 1862, Lincoln said:

[17] *Ibid.*, Vol. VIII, p. 174.
[18] *Ibid.*, Vol. VIII, pp. 217-218.

"You all may recollect that in taking up the sword thus forced into our hands, this government appealed to the prayers of the pious and the good, and declared that it placed its whole dependence upon the favor of God. I now humbly and reverently, in your presence, reiterate the acknowledgment of that dependence, not doubting that, if it shall please the Divine Being who determines the destinies of nations, this shall remain a united people, and that they will, humbly seeking the Divine guidance, make their prolonged national existence a source of new benefits to themselves and their successors, and to all classes and conditions of mankind." [19]

To a Methodist Conference he wrote:

"By the help of an all-wise Providence, I shall endeavor to do my duty, and I shall expect the continuance of your prayers for a right solution of our national difficulties and the restoration of our country to peace and prosperity." [20]

To a Baptist Society he also wrote:

"I can only thank you for thus adding to the effective and almost unanimous support which the Christian communities are so zealously giving to the country and to liberty. Indeed, it is difficult to conceive how it could be otherwise with any one professing Christianity, or even having

[19] *Ibid.*, Vol. VII, pp. 154-155.
[20] *Ibid.*, Vol. VII, p. 164.

ordinary perceptions of right and wrong. To read in the Bible, as the word of God Himself, that 'In the sweat of *thy* face shalt thou eat bread,' and to preach therefrom that, 'In the sweat of *other men's* faces shalt thou eat bread,' to my mind can scarcely be reconciled with honest sincerity. When brought to my final reckoning, may I have to answer for robbing no man of his goods; yet more tolerable even this, than for robbing one of himself and all that was his. When, a year or two ago, those professedly holy men of the South met in the semblance of prayer and devotion, and, in the name of him who said, 'As ye would all men should do unto you, do ye even so unto them,' appealed to the Christian world to aid them in doing to a whole race of men as they would have no man do unto themselves, to my thinking they contemned and insulted God and his Church far more than did Satan when he tempted the Saviour with the kingdoms of the earth. The devil's attempt was no more false, and far less hypocritical. But let me forbear, remembering it is also written, 'Judge not lest ye be judged.' " [21]

In September, 1864, Lincoln again wrote to Mrs. Gurney:

"I am much indebted to the good Christian people of the country for their constant prayers and consolations; and to no one of them more than to yourself. The purposes of the Almighty are per-

[21] *Ibid.,* Vol. X, pp. 109-110.

fect, and must prevail, though we erring mortals may fail to accurately perceive them in advance. We hoped for a happy termination of this terrible war long before this; but God knows best, and has ruled otherwise. We shall yet acknowledge his wisdom and our own error therein. Meanwhile we must work earnestly in the best lights he gives us, trusting that so working still conduces to the great ends he ordains. Surely he intends some great good to follow this mighty convulsion, which no mortal could make, and no mortal could stay. Your people, the Friends, have had, and are having, a very great trial. On principle and faith opposed to both war and oppression, they can only practically oppose oppression by war. In this hard dilemma some have chosen one horn, and some the other. For those appealing to me on conscientious grounds, I have done, and shall do, the best I could and can, in my own conscience, under my oath to the law. That you believe this I doubt not; and, believing it, I shall still receive for our country and myself your earnest prayers to our Father in heaven.'' [22]

In such interpretations and beliefs Lincoln had the support of the pious convictions and the faiths of the ecclesiastical societies of the Northern States.

In passing, it may be said that Lincoln, on grounds of either law or piety, had little concern

[22] *Ibid.*, Vol. X, pp. 215-216.

with that class of citizens known as "conscientious objectors." The Northern men who found themselves for ethical reasons unable to support the Government were few in number and small in influence. Quakers fought in the ranks. Philadelphia, their chief city, and not far from the field of the war's chief battle, was loyal to the Union cause.

The war was prolonged far beyond the thought of either contestant. The first call for Northern troops was for a term of service of only three months. The Southern States, like the German, believed that the adequacy of their preparation would compel a victory immediate and complete. But from the first defeats of the North in the middle months of '61, the conflict advanced, through McClellan's constant and vain promises of victory and subsequent defeats of '62, through the defeat of Lee at Gettysburg, the fall of Vicksburg, and the Shenandoah Valley triumph of the summer of '63, unto the final grapple of Grant and Lee, unto Sherman's march from Atlanta to the sea of '64 and '65, and finally unto the gradual and inevitable weakening of the Confederate forces, the curtailing of the field of operations, the cessation of hostilities, and the final surrender of Lee to Grant in April of '65.

The first two years of the present war were not unlike the first two years of the American conflict. The attacking party in the Civil War had the advantage; the attacking party in the World

War had the advantage; the attacking party usually has the advantage. But the nation attacked, especially if it be in either form or reality a republic, presently finds itself, and it finds itself the more completely and adequately the longer lasts the struggle. Throughout the second half of the four years of the American struggle it became more and more evident with each passing month that the Southern cause was weakening, the Northern strengthening, and that victory for the Northern eagles was becoming assured. Reverses for Lincoln's men were not unknown; but the sweep of the current was clear and its general force unstemmed. To point out the analogy would be superfluous.

Throughout the four years of the American contest attempts at peace were from time to time made. Not a few of such endeavors had their origin in the thin brains and soft hearts of unworthy philanthropists. Such men failed to perceive the essential relationships of the war, or to feel in particular the grip which the struggle against slavery had taken of the New England conscience. Several of these peace proposals were based on compromises—the compromises usually being a restoration of the conditions obtaining before the outbreak of the war: the seceding states to reënter the Union bearing their slaves with them. To all such intimations Lincoln gave a hearing as responsive as a patient mind and a humane heart could offer. For he knew the meaning of war, and of its continuance. But after the issue of the Emancipation Proclamation, which took effect at the beginning of the year '63, it became impossible to coöperate in any movement for peace which presumed upon the perpetuation of the South's "peculiar institution." Not only must the Union be preserved, but slavery must remain abolished.

The South desired peace; the North desired peace. But the terms proposed in correspondence, or in personal conferences—one of which Lincoln himself attended,—were not satisfactory. Seldom did the Commissioners come into close relations. The war had to be fought out—fought out unto the exhaustion of one of the contestants. No other conclusion seemed possible.

Is it not probable that the history of the American War of 1861-65 may prove to be a prophecy of the European War of 1914-16-17 in respect to its conclusion? All the warring nations desire peace. But the purposes for which England and her Allies are fighting cannot now be gained in the diplomats' council-chamber.

As I have intimated, the evidence became increasingly conclusive, in the last year of hostilities, that the seceding states would be finally and overwhelmingly defeated. Under this belief the problem of their readjustment to the whole national commonwealth became imminent. To this problem of reconstruction Lincoln was, however, called to give little heed. It became the question which, for the decade following the capitulation at Appomattox the National Congress, the President, the Judiciary, and the Government of the several states concerned were obliged to address themselves. Lincoln's death in April, 1865, freed the great President from seeking to understand and to do a duty more comprehensive, more perplexing, and more prolonged than the duty of saving the Union by force of arms. But before his passing, Lincoln, in the case of certain States whose territory had been won back, had intimated certain principles or methods touching the reconciliation of the rebelling states. That the application of these principles became impossible was an historic calamity.

These principles and methods were characteristic of the man himself. In them, as in him, are found no hint of retaliation. If ever there was a commander of armies and navies free from vindictiveness, that commander was Abraham Lincoln.

It was Lincoln who, as late as February, 1865, urged the payment of $480,000,000 to sixteen slave states on the basis of their former slave populations. It was he who in the following month, in the second inaugural address—one of the greatest of his State papers,—urged that the wounds of the *whole* nation be healed. It was he who more than a year before the close of the war wrote the common-sense judgment: "On principle I dislike an oath which requires a man to swear he has not done wrong. It rejects the Christian principle of forgiveness on terms of repentance. I think it is enough if a man does no wrong hereafter." [23]

In the last year of the war he indicated under many forms the gracious largeness of his spirit and his desire for a proper peace. Speaking of his second election, he said:

". . . It adds nothing to my satisfaction that any other man may be disappointed or pained by the result. May I ask those who have not differed from me to join with me in this same spirit toward those who have?" [24]

"He had once before said, but would say again," as reported in an interview, "that those who have differed from us and opposed us will see that the result of the presidential election is better for their own good than if they had been successful." [25]

He also wrote to Horace Greeley, the editor of the leading Republican paper:

"If you can find any person, anywhere, professing to have any proposition of Jefferson Davis in writing, for peace, embracing the restoration of the Union and abandonment of slavery, whatever else it embraces, say to him he may come to me with you; and that if he really brings such proposition, he shall at the least have safe conduct with the paper (and without publicity, if he chooses) to the point where you shall have met

[23] *Ibid.*, Vol. IX, p. 303.   [25] *Ibid.*, Vol. X, p. 271.
[24] *Ibid.*, Vol. X, pp. 264-265.

him. The same if there be two or more persons."[26]

An announcement concerning terms of peace, which was made 18th July 1864, reads:

"*To whom it may concern:* Any proposition which embraces the restoration of peace, the integrity of the whole Union, and the abandonment of slavery, and which comes by and with an authority that can control the armies now at war against the United States, will be received and considered by the executive government of the United States, and will be met by liberal terms on other substantial and collateral points, and the bearer or bearers thereof shall have safe conduct both ways."[27]

Such a policy of amnesty and of reconciliation may well be noted by any nation which is now at war, and which is proving to be a victor along a far-flung battle line in space and in time. It is ever to be remembered that our present enemies are to become our friends and co-workers in a mutual service for our common and needy humanity.

One and one only character emerges from the greatest of civil wars as a consummate contribution to the imperishable human wealth of the centuries. Grant, the commander in the field, by per-

[26] *Ibid*, Vol. X, p. 154.
[27] *Ibid.*, Vol. X, p. 161.

sistence and strategy brought the war to a victorious conclusion. Lee, recognized by the North as well as by the South as a great general and a great gentleman, throwing his sword into the scales of his beloved Virginia, was, and is, judged as true to the dictates of his conscience. Seward, Chase, Fessenden, Stanton, in foreign, financial, and military folios, did their executive duty. But humanity, like republics, has a short memory and a narrow vision. No one of them makes a universal or a lasting appeal. Lincoln towers above them all, uniquely great, and seems to loom up yet greater as the decades pass. Uneducated in the schools, he yet possessed that judgment which is the choicest fruit of the tree of knowledge, and that political wisdom which Burke defines in familiar phrase and incarnates in himself. Knowing few books, those few were each the "lifeblood of a master-spirit," the Bible and Shakespeare being chief. Knowing few men, till he became President, yet from those few he learned much of those conditions which help to form character, to discipline judgment, and to influence conduct. Called to bear tremendous responsibilities and to meet sudden emergencies, he had patience with himself, and also with his allies and his foes, in these unique crises. Strong in himself, and in a sort of semi-conscious knowledge knowing himself to be strong, he was humble in his own self-estimate and modest in bearing. With much to distract his attention and to exhaust his energy, as a true pilot he kept his eye and his heart upon the port to which he sought to bring the Ship of State. Avoiding the perils of the course of each day, he yet never forgot that other and future day—and at times apparently far-off—when the voyage should be done. Accused in the first years of the war of being slow, he was willing to wait, for he desired to carry his people with him— that necessary help to any executive: for prudence was his birthright and also a crowning virtue and grace. By might of arms he won; yet he knew that ideas, sentiments, convictions are the controlling forces among men, and that arms are only the lesser and temporary expressions of principles and emotions. He was obsessed with no theory of the State as a Superhuman Despot, ruling the individual, indifferent whether it crushes or ennobles; but he lived, loved, and died for a Union of States which was composed of individual freemen. Without the graces of face, form, or manners, he won his great way by the light of a large reasonableness, by the persuasiveness of a warm and big heart, by the majesty of a pure conscience, by a supreme faith in God, and by devotion to the service of God's little children. He was a genuine Shepherd of the People, so called by the greatest of American preachers, and he fed his human flock, and led them forth by right ways into a land of free habitations.

Not as yet, be it said, has the present war brought forth any character at all comparable to the Lincoln whom the American War created. If the present conflict has elevated some, it has not lifted them far; and others, quite as numerous, it has depressed. What the following year, or years, may bring forth in human leadership now rests in the lap of the gods.

As I bring this long comparison to a close, I find at least one reflection pressing for utterance: it is the belief that, at the conclusion of the present struggle—unspeakable as is the loss of life, lamentable as in the destruction of material accumulations, disheartening and perplexing as is the disintegration of the ordinary and orderly processes of civilized life,—the disintegration will prove to be less fundamental and less lasting than at the present moment seems certain, and the destruction of material values will be replaced with a completeness and a swiftness which now seem incredible. The sorrows of death can for many be removed only by the death of those who do sorrow. The experience of the North in the American War is the basis for such assurances. The soldiers returning fell naturally into their former conditions, vocations and professions. The farmer who had left his field came back to his plough and his reaper; the clerk to his old desk and counter; and the carpenter again took up his saw and his plane at the same well-worn bench. A currency vastly inflated gradually shrank to its legitimate proportions. Without jar or hindrance the forces of civilized order and orderliness resumed their wonted functions. Such was the case in the victorious North. In the defeated, sorely damaged, and much distressed South the condition was very different. In our analogy the North represents England and her Allies. For the victors in the Great War the prospect of the restoration of life's orderly processes at the signing of treaties of peace is far brighter, far more reassuring, than some Cassandras, be they never so wise and just, would have us believe. Those processes may not return to just what they were before, but they will be large, vital, happy though marred, constant, enlarging, enriching, progressive and finally triumphant.

VI

PROSPECTS OF LIBERAL EDUCATION AFTER THE GREAT WAR[*]

The writer of the Hebrew Psalm cxxxix. has given a good definition of a liberal education:

"Whither shall I go from thy spirit? or whither shall I flee from thy presence?

"If I ascend up into heaven, thou art there; if I make my bed in hell, behold, thou art there.

"If I take the wings of the morning, and dwell in the uttermost parts of the sea;

"Even there shall thy hand lead me, and thy right hand shall hold me."[1]

The glorious verses represent freedom of the mind. The picture is of the mind entering into wide realms of observation, passing into and through zones of experience, coming to know and to feel relationships, and appreciative of and responsive to deep and diverse contrasts. The mind is made to appear in its liberty either as the bird on the wing in the air, or as the fish of firm fin in the sea.

Education is called liberal because it is a liberator. It constitutes freedom. It gives to the mind

[*] April, 1918.
[1] Ps. cxxxix 7-10.

a sense of being at home in any proper society, and it offers to the mind a citizenship in every clime. Liberal education stands as a cause of the international mind. It creates a mind free from parochialism and provincialism. Liberal education stands for knowledge. But the knowledge is a sense of appreciation rather than a knowing of simple facts. Yet the mind is unwilling not to understand things as they are. For it does appreciate accuracy. In the subject of history, the man of liberal education would not suffer inaccuracy in a statement of facts. Yet he would be more intensely eager to point out the relations of these facts. In the subject of economics, he would seek to understand phenomena as separate and definite pieces of knowledge. Yet he would also, and possibly more devotedly, seek to relate these phenomena to each other and to all forms of knowledge—scientific, linguistic, philosophic, æsthetic. In the sciences—chemical, biological, geological, physical—the man of liberal education would emphasize the importance of seeing things as they are, and of making computations. But he would also devote himself to knowing the relations existing between chemistry and physics, between geology and biology, between biology and physics, between geology and chemistry. In the subject of logic, he would know the worth of the familiar forms of the syllogism. He might even know the doggerel which has come down to us from the schoolmen. But he would be yet more interested in the logical process as a method of the working of the human mind. In literature, he would know the methods and the motives of the schools of writing, and the limitations of the periods and zones. But he would be more deeply concerned with poetry and essay, with drama and history, as the noblest expositions of the imagination and of the heart of man.

Liberal education is fittingly contrasted with what is called an education for efficiency. Efficiency is interpreted in terms material. It represents values that can be seen, heard, touched. It stands for weights and measures. Its tools and signs are yardsticks and balances. It embodies the lust of the flesh, the lust of the eyes, and the pride of life, temporal and physical. It represents a civilization which makes for life's material comforts, for life's material splendors, for life's material forces, conditions, causes, results, and rewards.

Let there be no depreciation of a material civilization. Let its place be properly and fully recognized. But let it be said, once and for all, that the education of efficiency, resulting in a civilization material, is in and of itself not a liberal education. It is not a setting free of the human mind. It does not grow wings. It forms no relationships.

I have written of a liberal education as a form and definition of the intellect. Such an interpretation is true, but it is also open to the charge of being narrow. For a liberal education belongs to man as a willing and ethical being, of affections and appreciations, of duties to be done, of rights to be enjoyed, of choices, significant and truthful, to be made. A liberal education is to purify the heart, not simply for the vision of God, as intimates one of the greatest of the beatitudes, but also as a power of seeing all things. A liberal education is to give strength to the will that the choices, which the enlightened intellect may distinguish and point out, may be grasped firmly. A liberal education is to ennoble and enlarge the moral nature, that the door of character may justly swing on its four-hinged virtues. A liberal education is to give dignity and appreciation to the aesthetic faculty, that man may not be a stranger and a foreigner in a world of beauty, of song, of picture, of architecture, of poetry. A liberal education is to give aspiration and faith to the religious nature of man, that the eternities and the immensities may minister to him, not only as a subject of this world, but also as a citizen of the universe. For an illustration of a character, formed under training quite unlike the modern, but which was essentially, in heart and will and character, a liberal education, I turn to the far-off picture which Xenophon gives of Cyrus. For Xenophon speaks not only of his wisdom and presence of mind, but also of his magnanimity and generosity, his considerateness, his helpfulness, and his courage; not only of his power as a tactician, but also of his humanity, his nobility, amiability, and sympathy; not only of his strength of intellect in managing affairs, military, commercial, and governmental, but also of his faith in the gods and of his belief in the immortality of the soul.

In passing it may also be said that the difficulty characteristic of the German nation in the last score of years, and at the present time, in respect to a definition and appreciation of a liberal education, has arisen by reason of the failure of professor and of student to interpret a liberal education as being more than intellectual. The German university has come to understand and to encourage, at least to a large degree, the intellectual side. It has given us knowledge. It has weighed the facts. It has sought to relate fact to fact, and truth to truth. It has come to undersand the syllogistic art. But it has failed utterly to be responsive to the ethical and religious relations of knowledge. It has failed utterly to appreciate the humane application of intellectual truth. It has not brought its knowledge into the heart! Its concepts have not gone down into the feelings and emotions. It has grown the bones of intellectual culture and power. But it has not increased and augmented the life, the heart, the ethical feelings and appreciations belonging to the individual and to the people. It has made a Frankenstein, and a Frankenstein is a monster, belligerent, destructive.

Such an education as I have thus sought, and

feebly, to interpret is hard to create and to maintain in any society of whatever origin or constitution. But it is especially hard to create and to maintain in a new society. For in a new society the elemental material forces and facts have a place rather primary. Forests are to be felled, fields to be cultivated, roads to be laid out, houses to be built, streams to be dammed, wells to be dug, potatoes and wheat to be raised, cotton and woolen factories to be built. These simple material forces are first to be created and used. The time, the strength, and the opportunity remaining for the fostering of a liberal education are slight. The honor due to the Puritans of Massachusetts Bay in founding Harvard College within less than a score of years of the landing of the Englishmen on these shores becomes, in the light of this interpretation, one of the wonders of modern history.

The whole modern world is essentially a new physical world. The forces, chemical, electric, physical, that have been discovered, interpreted, and applied, have made this old world of ours a new world. And all this has been done, or largely done, within a hundred years. The application of steam to the transportation of personal property on sea and land; the invention of agricultural machinery; the discoveries of electricity, and the application of electricity to sending words, the human voice, light and heat, both with and without wire; the discovery of the Bessemer process, and of other processes, of making steel; the use of steel and of cement in the structure of buildings; the discovery of the phonograph, and the use of the forces that go to make up the moving picture; the use of the armored warship and of the submarine and of the air machine—have made this old world of ours, within a single lifetime, a new world.

In this new world the cause of liberal education has inevitably suffered. We have been so interested in and concerned with facts that we have lacked strength to see and to point out the meaning of facts, or to do the duty which the significance of facts might reveal. Our civilization rather has been material, physical.

I cannot but believe that this material condition is to receive special emphasis in the decades that shall follow the war. The physical world is still to be upon us. The process of discovery and the application of the results of discovery of nature's forces is to continue. As iron ships have in a generation supplanted the wooden, as the steel ships have supplanted the iron, as the steam railroad train has supplanted the stagecoach, and as electric trains have supplanted the steam, so also air machines may supplant or are supplanting earthly forces. In economics, too, a subject which is a bridge between the world material and the world intellectual in its content, the great principles of free trade and of production will undergo reëxamination. The doctrines of industrialism and of commercialism will be recast. For better or for worse, socialism will occupy a large and perhaps the largest part of the thinking of the human brain. The contrasts of poverty and of wealth, of opportunity and of limitation, may not become greater, but they will certainly become more significant. The whole world—material, economic, intellectual, physical—will apparently be flung into the melting-pot, and in the melting-pot it may become a seething mass, so fierce will be the fires of man's underlying and under-burning desires.

Under such a condition there is reason to fear that the cause of liberal education will be obliged to fight for its very existence. The impression easily comes to prevail that a liberal education does not amount to much anyway. For, it will be said, that forces material and forces purely and narrowly mental have been the chief powers in the present human overthrow. German university professors, who ought to have weighed evidence and examined facts, and reached the proper conclusions, based on principles and not on *ipse-dixit,* have been voluntary or involuntary liars. It will be said that culture has been sunk into kultur, and that this people, thus victimized, whose education Matthew Arnold clearly interpreted and warmly commended to his countrymen, have proved to be Huns. "If this be the result of a liberal education, we will have none of it," says the American. "If this be the conclusion of the whole aim of university training, we will convert our libraries into munition factories, our dormitories into barracks, our commons into messes. We will commission our professors as major-generals and our instructors as chiefs of ordnance."

It may, of course, be argued that the trouble is not with German education itself, even of the liberal type, but with the nature of that education. Its intellectual content was admirable, its purpose devilish. "Give us," says the liberalist, "the content, eliminate the hellish purpose, give us the right interpretation, and we will still keep the world true to liberalism, classical and scholarly, as well as political and civil." The argument is sound and should be urged. Yet, however persuasive the presentation, it is to be feared that an impression of narrowness and of hellishness will still prevail in some minds and influence some wills.

The cause of liberal education, following the close of the war, will also be obliged to meet the condition of diminished demand for members of several of the chief professions. The demand for architects and for physicians will, in my judgment, be increased rather than diminished. New structures should be built, and old ones and damaged ones repaired. Humanity, too, will be crippled and enfeebled, needing all hygienic services. The demand, however, for lawyers, for clergymen, will decline. The outer doorway to these two professional educations has been through the liberal college. The decline in demand will create a decline of interest in the great instruments and conditions of liberal learning. Of course it may be said that if there be a decline in demand, there also would be a decline in the number of men who can meet the demand. The loss of men, the great, the outstanding men, has been tremendous. The best were the first to respond to the call to the colors, and the best have fallen. The number of such men who are found in the list of writers is astounding. Take, for instance, the names of the poets who have fallen. The bare list of them gives a sense of *chokiness*. First and foremost is Rupert Brooke, whose poetry, of singular beauty and vigor, shows the quickening and the inspiring influence of the great war on English verse. His name may be followed by that of Julian Grenfell, about whose life and poetry it has been said that "there is something of the spiritual Titan"; Viscount Andrew John Stewart, of whom those outside his family and friends knew little until the great conflict gave wings to his thought; Charles Hamilton Sorley, who was killed about a month after Stewart, a youth of twenty-one, one of the youngest of the poets, whose verse, filling but one small volume, mutely testifies to the great loss to mankind in the premature silencing of his song; Robert Sterling, by whom in dying was won the fame which in times of peace might have been long in coming; H. Rex Freston, whose thought has been moved by the war into expression of undying words; Alan Seeger, a gift from the poets of America, whose poems, and diary and letters, published since his death, have given him in the heart of England a place which rivals that held by Rupert Brooke; Alexander Gordon Cowie, only twenty-two, but already a writer of poems of great beauty; Alfred Victor Radcliffe, a poet and a critic, a lover of nature, whose poetry shows both delicacy and vigor; Brian Brooke, who gave up his life in the first day's advance in the battle of the Somme, as did also W. N. Hodgson, another poet; Leslie Coulson, of great promise; and many others. This list of names, gathered by one of my colleagues, Mr. Walter Graham, is its own threnody.

But this loss is simply an intimation of the loss suffered among physicians and lawyers, and architects and other men of liberal sympathies and callings. Each name seems to be a stone in Valhalla. In another field, too, the cause of liberal learning will suffer, and suffer direfully, because of the scarcity of men, a scarcity caused not simply by the direct ravages of the war, but also because of the great financial rewards belonging to a life of research spent in industrialism. An American teacher, Julius Stieglitz, President of the American Chemical Society, in an address to his associates given at Boston, in September, 1917, said:

"Unless prompt measures are taken, we shall witness in a few years such a dearth of first-class tried material for professorships, that second-rate men will be placed where the national welfare needs the best we have, and third- and fourth-rate men will be occupying positions in which we should have young men of the highest promise in the period in which they are reaching full maturity. Indeed, it is greatly to be feared that even now we are witnessing a gradual lowering of standards. It would be futile to appeal to our industries not to call the men they need, although in the not distant future they will suffer most severely from the situation which is developing, if the present tendency remain unchecked.''

Yet notwithstanding all these sad and sinister interpretations, it is to be said that humanity has a certain way of repairing its damages and of doing away with the ravages wrought upon and by itself. Like the forests losing their first growth, there springs up a second one, which perhaps may be not so large and lusty as the first, but which also serves great uses. Within a hundred years, and sometimes within a shorter period, the damage wrought is apparently largely overcome. The intellectual condition is akin. It may be even better than that which originally obtained, or which might have obtained. The half-century which has elapsed since the close of the Civil War in America was a sad half-century for the Southern States which were devastated and whose social constitution was changed by the war. But the close of the fifty years gives to all America a higher stage of development than that which obtained in the year 1861. One believes that the cause of liberal learning cannot, and shall not, enter into a decline that shall prove to be permanent.

The disorganization to which I have already referred will not apply to the general community only. It will belong also to the cause of liberal learning itself. The staid and orderly processes, which have characterized the content and the progress of liberal learning in the past, will be maintained, but maintained only with great difficulty. Its content may become narrow and made thin. Signs of such disorganization are found in such a statement as was recently made by the president of an American college to its graduates. The President of Tufts College, speaking to the alumni living in Boston, said:

"Our present courses of instruction must be changed, and our enjoyment of the blessings of peace must be suspended. Our courses in history must concentrate attention on the present; our instruction in economics must busy itself with the vital problems of the day; our courses in biology must develop around the activity of the human body in health, in adversity, and in disease. Our courses in geology and mineralogy should leave the palæozoic and move up to the fuel, steel, and copper problems of now. Our French should prepare for the mud of Flanders; our German, for the quick understanding of the inventions of the enemy. Our mathematics should be used for a specific purpose; it is not a time for pure mathematics, pure science, pure art, or purity in any subjective form. It is a time when, in order to save these and many other precious things, we have to get into the grim work of war.''

Yet the disorganization of the American community and of the cause of liberal learning itself is to be accompanied by at least one mighty conservative, uniting and codifying, force. This force is found in the closer political union of Great Britain, France, and the United States. This union is sure to have a fundamental influence on the higher education in the newer nation.

At least three distinct periods in American education, as affected by foreign influences, are easily distinguished. The first, of course, was the English. The English was succeeded by the French, which, beginning soon after the close of the Revolutionary War, ended with the earlier decades of the nineteenth century. The French period, in turn, was followed by the German, which, beginning not far from 1830, continued down to the beginning of the twentieth century. Aside from the severance wrought in August, 1914, the influence of the German university over the American was, in the first years of the twentieth century, subsiding. But for threescore years and ten that influence was regnant. It has now, however, ended, and ended not to be resumed.

The higher education in America will at once return to its earlier allegiance. Yet the influence, exerted by Oxford and Cambridge and the Sorbonne, will not, in my judgment, become prevailing. But it will be pervasive. The new forces of the Rhodes scholarships have come to America, and will continue. The interruption of the present appointments will prove to be only temporary. The effect of the Rhodes men returning to America has been scholarly, humanizing, and has extended throughout the country. The presence of these men has served to eliminate the German point of view, and to cast out a certain narrowness of scholarship which is liable to belong to forces of purely American origin and advancement. Even if the Rhodes scholars have not persisted in academic work,—and about one-half have not persisted—yet their influence has tended towards the adoption of high scholastic ideals and towards the incorporation into our American system of high educational measures. Yet it is to be confessed that the number of Rhodes men who return to teach is not large in proportion to the whole constituency of an academic faculty. The Americans who go to Oxford and Cambridge, at their own charges, will never be large. Their influence, however, will be pervasive, though not spectacular.

A similar condition, *mutatis mutandis,* will obtain in respect to France. The American student should go to France for studies other than the Romance tongue and literatures. But the present outlook is not auspicious.

It is also to be said that the effect wrought by

the exchange professorships is good as far as it goes. But it never goes very far. These effects have their chief value in their by-products, rather than in their direct results. They serve to create an atmosphere of good feeling, not only academic, but also and more, international. After all, the scholarly work done in the university must ultimately and largely depend upon the regular incumbents.

In general, it is to be said, and said strongly, that the closer political union and fellowship of the three great nations is to prove to be a steadying and uplifting force in maintaining the higher intellectual and scholarly standards of the newest of the three peoples.

But in the years immediately following the war, and in the subsequent decades, liberal education, in order to maintain itself, and even to increase its force, should, in my judgment, give special heed to certain great, constant factors and elements of its learning. Among them I name history, literature, philosophy, and religion.

It is the tendency in a new country and in this new world of ours to live in, and to appreciate only, the present. Humanity is so little inclined to gather up experiences! It repeats its mistakes. It learns no lessons, or it learns them very feebly. Its progress is slow. History, therefore, has, or should have, a special meaning. Its records of the past should prove to be present-day pamphlets. It should have a meaning for the years, in which one lives, similar to that which Grote said he wanted his history of Greece to have in and for his England.

The worth of history as an element of liberal learning for the future becomes the more significant because of the enlarged interpretation and the more facile method of the historian. History, it is commonplace to say, has ceased to be largely political, and has become social. It has come to touch the bosoms and the businesses of men, as well as their cabinets and their coalitions. It has come to interpret Pope's line, in which one might make the change and say "that the proper history of mankind is man." This method becomes also the more pregnant with meaning if one thinks of history as the daily newspaper, only enlarged and filled with evidences more carefully arranged, with atmospheres and conditions more thoroughly weighed and appreciated, with conclusions more logically thought out. At its worst, the newspaper is quite as bad as anything can be. At its best, the newspaper is a moving history, and becomes material of and for lasting values.

In passage after passage Burke intimates the worth of history. In his *Reflections* he says: "In history a great volume is unrolled for our instruction, drawing the materials of future wisdom from the past errors and infirmities of mankind."[2] And again, he says history "is a great improver

[2] *Writings and Speeches of Edmund Burke* (Little, Brown and Co.), Vol. III, p. 418.

of the understanding, by showing both men and affairs in a great variety of views. From this source much political wisdom may be learned,—that is, may be learned as habit, not as precept,—and as an exercise to strengthen the mind, as furnishing materials to enlarge and enrich it."[3]

The philosophical and political biographer of Edmund Burke has, in a moving passage, indicated the same great interpretation. In the formal document by which John Morley transferred Lord Acton's library to the University of Cambridge, he said: "The very sight of this vast and ordered array in all departments, tongues, and times, of the history of civilized governments, the growth of faiths and institutions, the fluctuating movements of human thought, all the struggles of churches and creeds, the diverse types of great civil and ecclesiastical governors, the diverse ideals of States—all this will be to the ardent scholar a powerful stimulus to thought."[4] Such is the worth of history in the human reconstruction.

In the worth of literature as a means for the reconstruction of ravaged humanity, one easily calls to mind its cosmopolitan character. It is not a little singular, and it is most impressive, that the four poems which would, by common consent, be accepted as the four greatest poems, are written in four different tongues. To this consumma-

[3] *Ibid.*, Vol. IV, p. 468.
[4] Viscount Morley's *Recollections*, Vol. I, p. 232.

tion the Greek contributes majesty, the Latin sweetness, the Italian beauty, and the English strength. The unlikeness in language is no more unlike than the division in the periods of time which separates the age of Homer from the century of Milton.

In this re-making German literature will have its place. In a time yet more reflective than the present, we ought to, and we shall, be able to restore to ourselves the greatest works of at least four of the greatest minds which God has given to the world, Schiller, Goethe, Kant, and Lessing, of whom, let me add, Kant has the richest meaning to many men.[5]

The cause of liberal learning should not neglect above all else philosophy. For philosophy is the essence of the sciences. It is the fundamental truth and the elemental truths which underlie every science and every form of learning. Begin-

---

[5] It may not be unfitting for me to quote verses written by Charles Hamilton Sorley, who laid down his life in this struggle, in which he says to Germany:

"You are blind like us. Your hurt no man designed,
And no man claimed the conquest of your land.
But gropers both through fields of thought confined
We stumble and we do not understand.
You only saw your future bigly planned,
And we, the tapering paths of our own mind.
And in each other's dearest ways we stand,
And hiss and hate. And the blind fight the blind.
When it is peace, then we may view again
With new-won eyes each other's truer form
And wonder: Grown more loving-kind and warm,
We'll grasp firm hands and laugh at the old pain,
When it is peace. But until peace, the storm,
The darkness and the thunder and the rain."

ning with man, it seeks to show man in relationships. It is as broad as man's widest thinking, as deep as man's profoundest reflection, as high as his boldest imagination. In it are included logic, and psychology, epistomology, metaphysics. It is divided and trichotomized as is proper. But in any one of its several forms, in all of its applications, it represents the supreme field and the most powerful force of liberal learning. It is the science of principles. It is the understanding of methods. It is wisdom in the abstract, and wisdom applied. In philosophy the human spirit finds the truth of its individuality as embodied in Descartes' *cogito ergo sum;* and also it finds the equally important truth of Kant's categorical imperative. Personal character devoted to duty under the force of love is the guiding star of humanity.

Perhaps I have used too strong words in thus characterizing philosophy. For these phrases, some would say, ought to be reserved for religion. Religion is, in turn, to be a chief force, and perhaps the chiefest, in the reconstruction of mankind and in the promotion of liberal scholarship. And what is religion?

Religion stands for the incarnation of the Divine Being. It represents God on the earth. It gives intimations of the infinite, the eternal, the universal. It stands for that spirit in man which differentiates him both from things and from brutes. Religion takes on the divine forms of truth, of duty, of widest, highest relations. It calls to its service prophets who proclaim its truths, priests who minister at its altars, scholars who read and interpret its holy books. The progress of pure religion means the progress of the community. The decline of pure religion means the declining of the community. The college gives itself to the education of men who shall be prophets true, priests devout and devoted, scholars wise. It realizes that, if the oracles be dumb, if the priesthood be corrupt, if the altar-fires are impure, or the scripture false, the whole community suffers in the degradation of mind, of conscience, of conduct, and of life. It recognizes that if it can have a share in the education of the saints and prophets, it is giving a sky to the life of the community, a sense of infinity in the midst of its minute finites, and a God to a world living in the lust of the flesh and of the eyes.

Religion, thus interpreted, is to become the mightiest force in the rebuilding of man. Intimations of its power are already appearing in the turning of the hearts of the French nation unto its fundamental truths and its deepest consolations.

To this quartette of great subjects, history, literature, philosophy, religion, and in the use of the elements of these great subjects, liberal education, in the decades following the close of the war, should especially address itself. No other forces are comparable to these. They are not only the *summa bona,* but they are also the *fortissima bona.* They represent the past: for they gather up the past most completely. They represent the present: for they draw and embody the forces which constitute the modern world. They are at once the powers and the materials, the humanities and the humanity, and even the divinity which shall shape our ends. Because they represent the eternal spirit of humanity of the past, they shall create the eternal spirit of humanity in the future.

But in securing these most precious results, there is one supreme force to which attention should be given, and that is the force of the teacher himself. It is the force which Socrates was, and which many a leader of humanity, in the twenty-five hundred years that have passed since the greatest of Greeks drank the hemlock, has incarnated. The teacher is himself the great force in education, liberal or other. And in the teacher, be it at once said, two forces are preeminent—personality and truth. The two forces and elements ought to be combined in every teacher, and, as they are combined fittingly and in greatest relationships, is determined the worth of the teacher. If personality be lacking, even if truth be present, the result is weakness, ineffectiveness. If truth be lacking, falseness and error prevailing, the stronger and the more impressive the personality, the baser and the more lamentable is the evil resulting.

Truth may be found in the book. "Veritas," written across the open pages of three volumes is the shield of the oldest American college. But the results of such volumes are not teaching. It is only when truth is incarnated in and poured out by the person, impressed by the person upon other personalities, is there teaching. Thence results life. One of the favorite figures of Socrates was that he was a "midwife." It is more easy for humanity to learn and to feel truth than to secure great personalities. But when, to the calling of the teacher, one can summon men of great personality in whom are found enthusiasm, faith, hope, resolution, love for men, the kindling of self-sacrifice, the moral value of high religion, the resoluteness of the noblest aims—the cause of liberal education is not only made safe, but also becomes aggressive, and bears the assurance of ultimate and complete triumph.

VII

PUBLIC OPINION IN THE UNITED STATES IN THE THREE YEARS: 1914-1917 [*]

THE structural principle of the American Government is democracy. The most characteristic feature of American society is democratic equality. The truth of Jefferson's Declaration is still manifest after almost a century and a half of the affirmations and application of its sublime platitudes. The political philosophy which is taught in the academic classroom, as well as accepted in the social clubs with knowledge and in labor-union halls with half-knowledge, is democratic. Religion, which is still a dominant force, recognizes the democratic fact and rule, not only in the dissenting Congregational and Unitarian Churches of New England, but also in the republican Presbyterian Churches of the central West. The growth of agnosticism and of impersonal or personal pantheism intimates that ignorance of the spiritual infinities is equally common and equally influential or powerless among all classes of mind and all kinds of conscience and of will. The current inclination to depreciate the past, or even to

[*] October, 1917.

cut oneself free from the great forces of Hellenism and of Roman law and imperialism, to live only in the present and to feel only the power and the promise of the recent and the modern, is an outcropping of the spirit of democracy. Individualism—an individualism which is one of the results of the French Revolution transplanted into the rich soil of American life,—passing over into Socialism by leaps and bounds, represents the spread of the same conquering movement, a movement of the growth and the meaning of which the American people are still largely ignorant. The wiping out of political party lines, or rather the mingling and commingling of partisan principles, policies, ideals, and methods, helps to carry forward the democratic atmosphere and feeling. The physical well-being of the people—a well-being which is embodied in a tight roof over the head, a fat chicken in the pot, a warm hearthstone for one's feet, and a shirt on one's back—illustrates and helps forward the great political and social cause of democracy.

It may also be true that the geographical situation of America contributes to the same results. The present area of continental America largely, and the future area comprehensively, lies in the vast section between the Alleghenies and the Rockies, a plateau of two thousand miles in width, drained by the Mississippi and the Missouri, in which the topographical variations are hardly discernible to the human eye. Levels geographical promote the making of levels social and political. The similarities in dress, in manners, in habits of life, in scales of income and of expenditure, are at once causes and results of similarities in government, in feelings, and in intellect. Neither can it be doubted that the swiftness of transportation of persons, of goods, and of ideas by post, by telegraph, by telephone, by radio, has helped forward the movement of a democracy united and triumphant. The education of the people, supported out of the public chest, beginning with the kindergarten, continuing through intermediate and higher schools, and ending with the undergraduate college or the professional school of law, of medicine, of theology, of architecture, of journalism, and of other professions, tends to create a nation in which the majority rules without irritating arrogance and the minority submits without humiliation. Mysticism, a sense of the infinities, of the immensities, of the eternities, interpreted in terms of the emotions, is still a strong though a limited force in American life. Mysticism results in essential democracy through the elimination of the accidents and incidents of ordinary time and of space. The race spirit, however, is strong in cosmopolitan America; yet the race spirit spells within its narrow racial limits democracy.

It was into the bosoms and businesses of such a democratic nation, numbering a hundred million persons, that of an August morning of the year 1914 were thrust the tidings of the long-prophesied European war. For three years these tidings have with each sunrise and sunset continued.

This thrusting of world-shaking news into the American mind has been achieved on the whole with fullness and fairness. The journals of each day, of the great cities at least, for the first three years have given first place to war news. Special correspondents have contributed special and general interpretations, and the organized press associations have given the best news service which has ever been given in a time of war. Such service has been the chief source of the people's information and the chief material for their resulting judgment and feeling.

In this triennium these judgments and feelings have suffered fundamental changes. The first impression—more a sentiment than an idea—was one of surprise. Out of a national calm which the assassination of the Austrian Archduke only briefly and superficially interrupted came forth astonishment and confusion. Following the feeling of surprise emerged inquiries: "Why? What is it all about?" For Europe is very far-off from America. Germany, Austria, Russia, and all Balkan provinces are remote from the thinking and knowledge of the ordinary citizen. Diplomatic relations play a small part in the judgment and emotion of the American man. For the first months this surprise and inquiry continued. It was of course accented by the invasion of Belgium and the advance toward Paris of the German armies. These emotions were succeeded by those of horror—horror in which surprise and astonishment too had their part. For it soon was made evident that the world was dealing with a Power not only of unexampled might but also of unexampled ruthlessness. The Bismarckian principle of force was being applied without the Bismarckian emphasis upon the imponderables and the invisibles. The *Lusitania* was the culmination, and the approval of the German Government of the sinking was if possible a further culmination of the proof of personal ruthlessness and of national iniquity. The sense of horror was followed by a conviction that Germany was willing to descend to a depth of national sin and of international crime which had formerly seemed unthinkable.

For it has been impossible for the American mind to understand or for the American heart at all to appreciate the destruction which the German armies were inflicting on defenseless communities and individuals, or to realize in either intellect or conscience the support which the German Government, either positively or passively, was giving to the perpetration of such outrages. Perhaps the Armenian and Syrian deportations and massacres moved the American soul more deeply than any other devastation. For the relationship with Armenia and Syria through the Protestant missions is intimate. Thousands of members, too, of both nations are found living and working in the larger towns of America.

The feeling of surprise, of inquiry, of irritation, of horror, thus grew into antagonism. From the first days the question had frequently been asked, "Shall we get into it?" For two years and more it seemed clear that the Government was determined to do all that it could to keep us out of it. So strong was the impression made on the people that the Government should keep out, that President Wilson and his advisers were condemned by many people for undue conservatism or for indifference. But, on the other hand, one of the causes contributing to President Wilson's reelection was the cry, "He has kept us out of war." But such a judgment was, I believe, more common with the less thoughtful part of the people. Gradually, however, in the last month of the last year and in the first months of 1917, antagonism hardened, and with the hardening was made bitter. The U-boat campaign, the revelations of the plotting in Mexico, the conspiracy to attack the United States on its southern boundary from Mexican soil, and to wrest some part of American soil for the benefit of Mexico and Germany, brought all feelings to a head. No Government at all worthy could do otherwise than what the American Government did: A state of war was declared to exist. To this declaration the American people at once gave and have continued to give an unexampled unity of support. No war has ever been entered into which so commands the hearty and general support of the whole body of the American people as does the present. The number of dissenters in the Spanish War of 1898, the number of Copperheads and of peace-at-any-price men in the Civil War, the number of doubters in the Mexican War of 1846, the number of opponents in the War of 1812, and the number of loyalists who fought against the colonists in the Revolutionary War of 1776-83 were far greater in each instance than the number of disloyalists in the present unspeakably greater struggle.

These changes have gone on among a people which it is difficult to interpret with an exactness or conclusiveness which would seem just. In a superficial zone American society is primarily emotional and secondarily intellectual. Going a little more deeply beneath the surface, American society is perhaps equally emotional and intellectual. Probing yet deeper, this same society reverts to its primary state of being more largely emotional than intellectual. If one should, however, be allowed to go a bit further in the analysis, I think it would be found that the people are largely intellectual. The American feels before he thinks, at least in any large way. When the first flash of feeling has vanished somewhat, he reflects; having reflected, he finds his meditations react upon his feelings, and that his thought often absorbs his feelings. How often have I seen bodies, both large and small, of men educated and intellectual swept away by great floods of feeling! But beneath such conditions, which cover the largest share of the people, are found dwelling a small body of men whose feelings play a small part in their personal organization or activity, who are chiefly forces and agents intellectual.

With all these sections and zones of American society the democratic movement has in the period under review gained, and gained in common with its spread throughout the world. The sublime sentiments of Lincoln regarding government of and for and by the people, spoken under unlike conditions and in diverse phrases, have never been more often repeated or made to connote richer or more inspiring meanings. In the United States, as elsewhere, democracy never goes backward, and usually advances. This increasing power belongs, in my judgment, rather more to the educated classes than to other parts of the community. The evidence for this opinion lies in the eagerness of these higher classes, as found in the colleges and universities, to respond to the call for service, military, naval, civil. The response has been quite as prompt and enthusiastic as it was in the Civil War, which of course came unspeakably nearer home. Not a few colleges have lost or are to lose one-half of their students in the next academic years. Football gridirons and baseball diamonds have become drill-grounds, dormitories barracks, gymnasiums armories, and commons messes. Such enthusiasm and response are what was expected, and even demanded, by faculties and trustees. To the democratic State, educational institutions are in debt for their existence. When the State is menaced they therefore should, and do, leap to her defense.

Among the middle classes, and especially in that part which might be called the lower half of the third estate, I do not believe the democratic sentiment has in recent years strengthened. A domestic and an individualistic, centrifugal movement has progressed. Its members, in their prosperity and comfortableness, are more inclined to ask, "What have we to do with Europe? Its problems and its difficulties and wars are not our concern. What, too, has Europe done for us that we should sacrifice for her? Have we not earned all that we have got?"

My reason for such judgment lies in the apathy under which the people seem to rest, and in the slowness with which they have responded to the call for enlistments in the army and navy made by the President. In a proper democracy the call for volunteers should be promptly and fully answered, and answered with overflowing enthusiasm, answered with a sense of privilege and of joyous entrance into an opportunity. The answer has been made with slowness and with indifference. In a proper democracy conscription should not be necessary. But conscription is necessary, and is now in the process of making. The democratic system has not furnished America with a proper number of volunteer soldiers. The army is largely a conscript army. Perhaps, however, one who would differ with me would say that democracies are not made to fight, and that martial standards do not form the proper test to apply to a democracy.

In this democratic condition, however, there is occurring a movement which has deep meaning for the present, and ultimately may have deeper meaning, for America and for the world. This movement is Socialism. Of the manifold definitions of Socialism, let me, in order to be clear, accept that definition which interprets Socialism as being a method of government in which the State performs functions for the individual which formerly he performed for himself. Under this definition, in the years immediately preceding the outbreak of the war and in the three years succeeding, Socialism has moved with tremendous strides, and was never moving more rapidly than at this moment. The transportation business is perhaps the more comprehensive field. The railroads have in the last month been largely commandeered by the Government. In its parcels post it has become the rival of the express companies. The owning and running of ships cover a similar field on water. The business of insuring the lives of its soldiers is a function formerly given over to the insurance societies. It has gone into the coal business in reference to the regulation of prices. It has for a generation or more been in the banking business through its system of national banks, but recently it has taken a much larger and more controlling hand in what is known as its Federal Reserve system. In part, and only in part, these measures are war measures, and by most would be confessed necessary. Their political function and place following the close of the war covers a more serious question, which thoughtful minds are already considering.

In all the thinking and discussion of these years, of course, the great arch-enemy has occupied the largest place. The public opinion about Germany has passed through several sea changes, and also, one may be suffered to add, several land changes also. The opinion, too, differs in different strata of the cosmopolitan population. For two and a half years the Germans living in America, either German-born or of German heritage, sympathized with their home people. This sympathy was voiced in many ways, the newspaper being the chief method. The German press of the United States is a many-voiced organ. The daily journals published in New York, Chicago, Cincinnati, Milwaukee, and other cities have not less than a million readers. The sinking of the *Lusitania* was regarded by them as a legitimate war measure. The victories of Germany have constantly been received with satisfaction and the victories of the Allies with depreciation. Their recent utterances have been less sympathetic, but the sympathy is still felt if not so fully expressed. Though the press is an exponent of public opinion, yet I do believe that the Germans who have chosen America as their home are more loyal to the country of their adoption than their papers intimate. Before the declaration of war was made, the Governor of New York said to me that three of the outstanding German citizens of the State offered, in case of a declaration of war between Germany and the United States, to raise a regiment of their own German citizens to fight against Germany. In general the loyalty of the German population can be counted upon, and yet, be it added, not with that full sense of enthusiasm which would belong to the native American citizen.

It should also be noted that on the part of most Americans is entertained no feeling of revenge against Germany. Of course, the outrages perpetrated by Germany, in Belgium, in Poland, and by its consent in Syria, Armenia, and other parts, have created the deepest emotion of horror. Yet there prevails no desire for reprisal. The feeling is one of pity for the outraged and of desire to give relief, and of pity also that a nation could so far forget herself as to be guilty of such devastation. In the first years thoughtful men made a careful discrimination between the Germany of Kant, of Schiller, and of Goethe, and the Germany of Bismarck, of the present Kaiser, and of their entourage; but as the years have passed it has become evident that the German people, either through misinformation or misinterpretation or ignorance or timidity, have stood with their Government in this war. Under this solidarity of judgment and of emotion the feeling of sympathy with and of regard for the Teutonic peoples has distinctly and greatly lessened. It may be added that their boastfulness has on the whole awakened the sense of the ridiculous, and also a sense of psychological inquiry regarding the origin and prevalence of such unique boastfulness and bumptiousness among a scholarly and thoughtful people.

Although no feeling of revenge prevails, yet deep antagonism does prevail which has taken on a minor form of more or less extreme silliness. The special form I have in mind is the elimination of the teaching of the German language and literature from schools and colleges. For many years German has been the most popular of all foreign languages in acadamic curricula. The beginning of this popularity occurred about forty years ago, and it has increased with each decade. But at the present time in the public schools of many cities it is proposed to eliminate the language as a subject of study. In the colleges the courses will still be given, but probably with considerable curtailment.

The opinion, however, is common that in one respect at least the United States was justified in going to rather extreme measures in retaliation. This respect relates, not to the U-boat warfare or to Belgium outrages, but to the representation of Germany in the United States. The suspicions for a long time entertained have now been proved to be true. Propaganda was on neutral American territory constantly and powerfully carried on by representatives of the German Empire. The promotion was done not only through money, but by methods deceitful, surreptitious, and insidious, by the destruction of property, by stratagem which caused the innocent to suffer with the presumed guilty and by violence resulting in the loss of life. It was all a nasty business done in the name of a great Power on neutral territory. The revelations were made after the recall of the German Ambassador and to his perfidy. Yet it was carried on with such clumsiness that it failed of its supreme purpose. Its chief result was to madden the American people and to unite them in the support of a declaration of war.

The opinions of the American people have been formed not only in regard to movements, diplomatic measures, and the doctrines of rights and duties, but also in regard to personalities. Of all personalities engaged in the great affair, no one has commanded the attention of thoughtful people more constantly or with warmer affection than Lord Bryce. For Lord Bryce, more commonly spoken of as Mr. Bryce, holds the deep respect and regard of the American nation. This feeling arises from general causes which create the regard and respect of all, but also from two special reasons: his service as ambassador, and his book, *The American Commonwealth*. His ambassadorship is interpreted in no narrowly diplomatic sense, but rather as a great friendship, educational and personal. He touched American life on many sides, and touched it only to enlighten, to enlarge, to enrich. The student found in the author of *The Holy Roman Empire* and in the Oxford Regius Professor of Civil Law a sympathetic teacher. The Congressman found in the author of *The American Commonwealth* a statesman who understood his own American problems quite as well as himself. The lawyer found in the writer of the *Studies in History and Jurisprudence* a mind rich, inquisitive, and constructive. The manufacturer and the merchant throughout the country discovered in Mr. Bryce an interpreter whose questions reached far down into surprising detail and upward into inductions to which they had given little or no heed. Mr. Bryce was indeed our great British friend; his presence was always most grateful and his addresses quickening and informing. He once said to me he had spoken in every State of the American Union, excepting only two or three.

At the beginning of the war the figure of Sir Edward Grey (as he then was known), emerged for the first time to the ordinary American mind. From this mind he has, for the time being, vanished. But the impression made in those first eventful days is to last. This impression is, that no man ever labored with greater earnestness, or with a heartiness more sincere or with a laboriousness more intense, in the promotion of the great end of peace. Not only the White Book, but every other Book when properly read, furnishes proof of the conclusion.

The American judgment of two other great Englishmen has also been made plain. The two can for my purpose be bracketed—Mr. Asquith and Mr. Lloyd George. Of Mr. Asquith the opinion has heightened in respect to his ability as a thoughtful statesman. It has fallen in respect to his ability as an executive. His ship is built, it is believed, to sail the broad calm seas of statesmanship, a ship bearing richest cargo, but one unable to breast swift and strong tides and hard storms, or to escape shoals and rocks such as it has met in these years. His retirement was inevitable. But, on the contrary, his successor is regarded as of a type very unlike. Mr. Lloyd George has come to be thought of as a statesman especially called to an increasingly lofty and critical duty. This duty he interprets with a certain narrowness not belonging to his predecessor, but also with a fearlessness and a force which were quite foreign to Mr. Asquith. Joshua succeeded Moses in the command of the chosen people. Although less great than the legislator, Joshua did what Moses could not do—he brought Israel into the promised land.

Concerning the two most outstanding Germans of the present or the last generation, American opinion has also suffered a change. Regarding Bismarck the change lies in rather a deepening of opinion than in alteration. The regard for his prescience has become greater. This prescience was manifest in his willingness not to demand the uttermost farthing of either blood, or treasure, or territory of the defeated foe, either of France in 1871, or of Austria in 1866. If his counsel had been followed in 1871, the present war might have been avoided at least for a time. But also the judgment has become confirmed that Bismarck is one of the ultimate causes of the present crisis. Through his insistence on making German welfare an ethical and political standard, he served to intoxicate the German mind with the notion of Germany's present and future greatness. His argument that what is good for Germany is good for all, what is bad for Germany is essentially bad, what is right for Germany is fundamentally right and what is wrong for Germany is fundamentally wrong, established a standard and a test which allowed and quickened the breaking of treaties, the forging of telegrams, and the declaration of war. His interpretation of Germany has helped the nation to sell its soul for a mess of pottage, fiery, liquid, red. Be it added, too, it is going to lose the pottage as well as, for the time being, its soul.

In the half-seen background is always discerned

by the American the sinister and helmeted figure of the Kaiser. In America, before his reign began and immediately after, there was felt a special prejudice against him, based partly on his treatment of his English mother and partly on his outstanding peculiarities. These peculiarities, it was believed by many, might bring his reign to a sudden end by his confinement in a sanitary schloss. But as the years and the decades have passed it has become evident that he was making himself more and more a master of his own will and of the will of others. His protestations that he was the peace-lord of the world came to be received with constantly increasing confidence. The marvelous commercial and industrial progress of the nation was due, at least in part, it was recognized, to his encouragement and initiative. It was also reasoned that the industrial and financial place which Germany had secured and was pretty sure to enlarge would prevent the Kaiser from entering into a great war.

The circumstances attending the outbreak of the war and the conditions of its waging have completely altered these interpretations. The heart and mind of the American people now are convinced that the real author and the real continuing force of the war is the Kaiser himself. Tales of the dominant influence of the war party and of his Majesty's reluctance in yielding to the pleadings and arguments of the war party have been received from time to time, but they have not served to becloud the real point of responsibility. The falsehoods of the military and civil authorities regarding affairs in Belgium and Poland and France have not for a moment beguiled the American people into the belief that these excesses could not have been avoided by a word from the throne. Journal after journal in American cities has printed indictments against him which would be sufficient to consign not a single guilty criminal, but a whole Prussian division, to punishment.

If one looks below the surface, the reason for the Kaiser's waging such a war by such methods lies in the Bismarckian formula touching Teutonic supremacy and the betterment for the world which is sure to result from such supremacy.

The judgment of the American people regarding certain personalities both in Germany and England becomes yet more emphatic when one considers the opinion which is entertained in America regarding England's share in the great undertaking. About the year 1893, on the anniversary of Perry's victory on Lake Erie, I heard a leading lawyer of a leading American city, with bravado in voice and manner, declare, "We have licked England twice, and we can do it again." It was of course a cheap piece of swashbuckling. That lawyer would not say now what he said then. He would not have made the remark in the past decade on any anniversary of Perry's victory. For the feeling of America toward England has shown a distinct decline of antagonism and a distinct increase of sympathy. The causes of the change have been general, belonging to commerce, to industry, to literature. The causes have been also in no small part personal. The presence of Lord Bryce on the one side, and on the other of Lowell, of Hay and of Choate, have proved the source of sympathetic interpretations and fellowship. But out of the war, even before the public declaration against Germany, a sense of peculiar oneness has taken the place of antagonism or of indifference. The uniting is now quite complete, for not only is America fighting with Great Britain for the world of democracy, but it is now plainly seen that Great Britain is fighting the battle of the world for democracy, not only worldwide, but also American. That thin, wavering, unconquerable red line in France and Flanders of October 1914 was what stood between not only a democratic and an autocratic world, but also what stood between a democratic America and a Germanized America. Great Britain fought the American battle in France in the summer months of 1914. If in 1776 and the years following Great Britain committed sins and follies against the American colonies, she has now made an atonement full and complete. The troops of George V. in France undid what the troops of George III. were guilty of in America a hundred and fifty years before.

Before America's formal entrance, as well as

after, the war struck a fundamental note in the character of the community and of the individual. That note is a religious one. For man is not only naturally religious, as a Church father said: He is also unconquerably religious. A crisis like the present flings the individual in thought and feeling back upon the infinite, the eternal, the universal. In the possibility that he may lose his body, man, the soldier, is inclined to ask whether he will keep his soul or whether he has a soul at all worth keeping. In the probability that some one of those dear to him will not return with the coming of peace, he inquires whether he will see his pilot face to face. "What is worth struggling for, what is worth living for, what is worth dying for?" is his persistent question. Individualism is tabooed, selfishness made impossible, the will to live becomes shameless. That truth is the worthiest object of one's thought, duty of one's endeavor, righteousness of one's struggle, honor of one's allegiance, and service of one's sacrifice, become inspiring sentiments and thrilling rallying-cries. In my city of Cleveland was recently held a meeting of more than three hundred of its chief business men. The assembly was a recognition of the raising in a week by voluntary offerings of more than four and a half million dollars for the Red Cross. A dozen brief addresses were made by merchants and manufacturers. The note prevailing in these speeches was a spiritual one: it was the note of God and of God's world, of the individual's and the race's duty to the Divine Person and to His creatures. The note thus struck is general and deep in the American character.

The formal Church recognizes this spiritual movement, but not fully; yet in recognizing it, the Church is not always able to adjust itself to these spiritual demands. The river of God is so full of water that the stream has overflowed its common banks of thinking and of devotional expression. The American Church has no personality like Phillips Brooks or Henry Ward Beecher to quicken and to direct its feelings. It is a personality and not a creed, be the creed never so wide or true, it is a personality not an organization, be that organization never so historic or complete, which is demanded by the heart of a nation in a national crisis.

In this spiritual and other experience through which America is now passing, even slight reflection brings to consciousness a sense of the unused strength of the people. A population of a hundred millions should of course have vast strength held in reserve, although one at once acknowledges that India's population is threefold and China's fourfold greater than America's. Mere numbers may constitute not strength but weakness. But this population, living under a stable republican, democratic government, with material property of uncounted billions and means of augmenting this property each year by an amount which most nations do not possess as their entire wealth, resting on a stable history of three hundred years, a people orderly, religious, intelligent, loyal to high ideals, has great forces in reserve. These forces are quite as much moral as they are physical. This fact of unexpended assets helps to explain the indifference of many Americans to evils in their body politic and in their individual souls, evils which seem to a foreigner rather menacing. The Americans, however, know that these evils—and they are free to confess that they are evils—are slight in comparison with the strength and virtue inherent and structural in American society. They also are willing to acknowledge that these evils they can remove whenever they make up their mind or their will to. This sense of reserve, moreover, may have close metaphysical relation with the self-restraint of the nation which has characterized its dealings with Germany during these last three years.

This consciousness of unused power has possibly some bearing on a question which, in the opinion of a few, is still awaiting decision: The question whether the evidence afforded by the war is for or against the value of great standing armies. America and England have not maintained great bodies of troops ready for service, yet in six months Kitchener's mob was converted into a fine fighting machine. In a scarcely longer period America will convert a million raw recruits into a compact, well-disciplined, well-equipped, victorious force—a force, which joining other forces, will help to conquer German's longstanding millions. On the whole, given a nation of physical resources and of intellectual and administrative resourcefulness, the evidence, even on the martial side, is against the policy of maintaining vast armies in times of peace.

In this struggle, as in other fundamental movements, have emerged two opposing tendencies: I refer to the individualistic and the racial or cosmopolitan. In the later part of this three-year period has sprung up with special vigor a movement for what is called Americanization. The movement embodies a desire to transmute all the members of all these diverse nationalities into Americans. The fire beneath the melting pot, always burning, has in these last days received fresh fuel. The importance of mobilizing all forces in the prosecution of the war has become recognized; therefore, not "America for the Americans" is the accepted doctrine—that is a too narrow interpretation,—but "all Americans" is the slogan. Not only is the campaign to naturalize foreigners, but also and more the endeavor is to inspire foreigners with the spirit of America, to acquaint them with American history, to instruct them in American traditions, and above all else to teach them to speak, to write, to think the American language, which, thank God, is the English tongue.

Yet, while this movement for Americanization has been going on, there has also progressed a world-tendency: a tendency to think in terms of the world and of all history. It is a tendency not only for the races, but also, and more, for the race. We have realized that above all nations is humanity. We have come to appreciate the truth that we must think in world-terms. We are to think cosmically. We have learned that no nation either liveth or dieth to itself. We have been taught to believe that the suffering of one finally becomes the loss of all, and the gain of one is the gain of all, and the gain of all is the advantage of each. We have now come to understand, as we have not understood, that the world's sorrows are America's griefs, the world's burdens America's weights, the world's degradations America's shame, the world's hopes America's assurances, and the world's victories—which are sure to be won—are America's triumphs.

VIII

AMERICAN SOCIETY AFTER THE GREAT WAR *

In the preface of his *Mixed Essays,* Matthew Arnold enumerates briefly the powers which, as he says, contribute to the building up of human civilization. "They are the power of conduct, the power of intellect and knowledge, the power of beauty, the power of social life and manners. Expansion, conduct, science, beauty, manners,— here are the conditions of civilisation, the claimants which man must satisfy before he can be humanised."

The paragraph is marked by the "sweetness and light" which characterize the interpretations made by the wise and tender-hearted critic of our manners, our books, our education, our theology, and indeed of our whole life. But at the present moment in America, life in its institutions, formal and permanent, seems to be brought under a criticism deeper and more thorough-going than that which Mr. Arnold in many instances gave. Our present questioning and our criticism relate to the constitution and not to the by-laws of our

* January, 1919.

complete and complex being. The questioning, too, touches the future, with either a promise or a foreboding, unlike that which the critic at once playful and serious adopted.

First in time and first in importance is the institution of the family. What is to be the human family in the decades following the close of the war? In this brief interpretation let me at once say in answer that the present position of the family as a social unit and agency will be influenced largely by the possible change in the so-called headship of the family. The change is made through a change in its economic status. The change concerns itself largely with the wife and the mother becoming a more important wage-earner. The family headship has been vested in the man by reason largely of his being the producer of the family income. The woman has been the spender, or the trustee, of the resulting revenue. This condition no longer so commonly or so fully obtains. The wife is now earning or can earn in many instances as much money as the husband.

This economic change is accompanied by the political change of the enfranchisement of women in many States. This enlarged function tends to emphasize the enlarged domestic freedom and function.

The narrower and the broader interpretations of this vast social revolution are a part of the movement for individualism, which has been progressing with ever-increasing swiftness since the

French Revolution of 1789. Against this stronger emphasis of individualism the American family, as a family, is to contend. But that the monogamous family will still remain as the great social unit is not to be questioned. Its place is firmly fixed in the history of civilization and in the heart of man. Neither the plural religious marriage of Mormonism, nor the polygamous State-marriage, nor the companionate marriage of society, can secure a footing at all lasting or broad. Each example of it will remain exceptional and sporadic. The heart of man abominates such doctrines and practices, and the same heart by instinct and training is devoted to the preservation of the highest and noblest instituton of society.

Regarding another institution the war is bringing to a head certain processes and conditions long operative. That institution is the Church. (Purposely I write of the Protestant only.) In thinking about the Church there are at least five points of interpretation. They are the churches, or denominations, the creed, the Bible, the clerical order and its relation to certain other organizations, and Sunday. In America the Church stands for the churches. There are, I believe, somewhat over a hundred and fifty different types or orders or eccleciastical denominations. They are based upon or determined by principles more or less fundamental, or upon fancies as trivial as buttons or hooks and eyes of personal apparel. The war is serving to bring the churches of the great faiths into more intimate affiliation and closer administrative co-working. In the light of the need of economic efficiency, the expense of much denominational individualism and support is seen to be nothing other than ecclesiastical extravagance or luxury or pettiness. In the light of fundamental principles, minor beliefs are recognized as unworthy of serious and large-minded men. It may also be added that the process going on in the different denominations, in the wiping out of sectarian differences, is also occurring within the churches of each individual faith. The change is found in the abolition of ecclesiastical rivalries and in the uniting of churches which, on the basis of geographical, religious, and social conditions, do belong together.

These closer affiliations are the result of both administrative conditions and of the lessening of differences in doctrinal formulas. The next centuries, if one may be allowed to prophesy for a very long time, are not to be, like the sixteenth century, centuries of the making of creeds or of the elaboration of theological systems. The specific articles of the great Confessions are to have less significance for the community. Doctrines so important even as the divinity of Christ are not to be made the subject of such prolonged thinking or the object of such emphasis in application as they have received in the remote or recent past. Definite theories of eschatology will come to be regarded almost as archæological specimens. But with such declines will synchronize an increase of emphasis on the great fundamental fact of religion itself. Religion will be based, as of course it always is primarily based, on a belief in a God, and on a belief in the duty of promoting human well-being. It will in fact include, and include not much more than, the two great commandments of Christ himself, or Micah's sententious threefold interrogations. Neither will the forthcoming faith question very deeply who or what is its God:— whether this God is to be interpreted as personal or impersonal; whether its Supreme One is to be spelled with a capital or a small letter. To us as individuals the old faiths will have lasting meanings and controlling values; but the community will employ the elective system in its theological adoptions. Whether the community shall adopt as its divine one the Power, not ourselves, that makes for righteousness, or Herbert Spencer's Unknown and Unknowable, or John Stuart Mill's obscure guess at divinity adopted in late life, or the Apostles' Creed, is a subject for its own consideration and selection. But, at all events, that religion which is accepted will be a religion which shall be at least a comfort to the human heart in life's sorrows, which shall give at least some guidance to the human mind in its questioning and doubting and bewilderment, and which shall be as the bread and the water of life for daily sustenance.

It would not be strange to find in such a revival

of deep religiousness an element of mysticism. The heart will come to assert itself more than ever as having reasons, as Pascal says, which the reason knows not of. Faith will have a meaning which, if unlike Paul's conception, will still possess a significance quite as forceful as that which the writer of the Epistle to the Romans gave to it in the upbuilding of human character. Religious confidences and confirmations will find themselves outstripping rational evidences. Already in that most rationalistic of all churches, the Unitarian, intimations of such a revival are felt.

A similar freedom will also be manifest in the beliefs about the holy books of the Church. For a generation the Bible has been the object of assault —textual, historical, dogmatic. Yet the Bible as a piece of noblest religious literature still stands, and will continue to endure. It will remain, at least in its New Testament, a worthy ethical and religious guide and interpreter. It will endure as an incomparable religious standard, because it bears to humanity the biography and the personality of Jesus Christ. Minor considerations concerning the Bible have dropped away, and will continue to be eliminated, only to emphasize the permanent essential element of the personality of Christ.

In every system of religion, pagan as well as Christian, sacred days seem to go along with sacred books. The integrity or the disruption of either serves to accentuate the integrity or the disruption of the other. The holy day of each week of the Christian Church seems almost to be a part of the question of the maintenance of the Bible itself. The old commandment of the 20th of Exodus, directing rest and worship, is interpreted by Christ's statement that the Sabbath is made for man, and not man for the Sabbath. Christ's statement in turn is liable in modern life to be interpreted in terms of man's pleasure or immediate convenience, rather than in terms of human and rational enrichment. In war many things are silent beside the formal laws, and many things become noisy beside cannon and ammunition wagons. The necessary preparation for war, the inevitable consequences of war, disrupt or destroy the physical, ethical, and other conditions which Christ's remark seems designed to promote. These consequences also take away the opportunity for worship which He by practice illustrated and by precept commanded. It is doubtful whether the old Sabbath, even in the form of the antebellum days, can be restored. Individualism will yet more deeply characterize the observance or lack of observance of the day. It may be said also that the Church and the clergy should find in such freedom of individual observance the richest opportunity for pressing their claims upon man—man who is still to be recognized as naturally Christian, or at least religious. What a chance for the great preacher!

The position of the clergy, furthermore, is to be

beset, as it already is beset, by at least two influences or human impressions. One is the impression that the profession has not quite done its proper part in the war. Its ministers seem to some observers to have nursed a "cloistered virtue" and its priesthood "has warmed itself at the fire." The impression, I believe, is thoroughly false. Historically, from the Middle Ages, the freedom of the clergy from bearing arms has had a good basis. The hand that administered the sacraments was not to be suffered to incur the risk of being stained with human blood. But the exemption from military service, given by the Government to the clergy and to the theological students, has made a false impression on the public mind. It has created the impression that the clergy either did not wish to bear arms or was unable to bear them. The fact is that the clergymen do wish to bear arms quite as thoroughly as do lawyers or architects or editors or teachers. A second influence besetting the profession lies in the growing belief among certain classes that the chief function of the calling, excepting the sacerdotal, may be taken over by the Young Men's Christian Association. Of course the Young Men's Christian Association is simply a federation of the churches. This comprehensive and commanding organization gets its power, personal and financial, from the churches. Without the churches, or the lay leaders of the churches, the Association could not live for a single day. But the community forgets the fact. It thinks of its "Y. M C. A." as apart from the churches, and at times as almost opposed to them. Such an impression is harmful, as it is contrary to the facts.

Another of the great human institutions will emerge from the crisis with certain parts weakened and other parts strengthened. I refer to the Government. The Government as a legislative fact or function will be less significant and influential. The Government as an executive force will be greatly strengthened. The judicial body still retains and will continue to retain its high place in the respect of the people. That body is our anchor; and it is an anchor which is attached, and properly attached, to the ship of State with a long and flexible cable. The causes of the weakening of the legislative and the strengthening of the executive force are manifold. But two causes seem to be chief. The decrease of the intellectual power of the typical legislator, and the absolute necessity of the executive force assuming special functions in a time of war, are perhaps the two most conspicuous causes of the change. This enlargement of executive power will in my judgment be easily continued and readily assented to by the people in the forthcoming time of peace.

Despite the increase of executive forcefulness, we are also to see a vast increase of what is known as Socialism. Accepting the definition of this undefined or ill-defined term as standing in its ultimate elements for the condition in which the community does for the individual what in many respects the individual did formerly for himself, one need have little fear of evil resulting. In fact the community has already become far more socialistic than it usually recognizes, and the community still exists, and the individual is still safe!

Alike by formal law and by judicial interpretation and executive application our Federal system is vastly to be extended. The increasing unity, the developing solidarity of the American nation in sentiment, commerce, education, industrialism, administration, are both cause and result of our stronger Federal system. What we call progress has helped Alexander Hamilton's principles and methods unto a complete triumph.

In respect to foreign commercial relations of the Government, America will find herself in much the same relation that Great Britain found herself in the middle of the last century—a condition in which a free-trade policy will make for commercial and industrial prosperity. This policy may be accompanied by a system of protection among lesser nations, or with a system of preferential tariffs with certain peoples more or less closely allied with the American State. Gradually, however, the free-trade method will come to obtain among all nations.

Business in its largest relations of making and exchanging goods is to see a vast development. The *vacua* which the war has created, abhorred by peaceful industrialism, will be filled up with unexampled rapidity and in probable confusion. The demand for labor and for capital, commanding as it now is, will become yet more insistent. Costs will mount up and all contributing forces which make for the increase in prices will be vastly magnified. To only one important element in this vast and complex field do I now wish to refer, namely, the relation of capital and labor. This relation, which by personal influence and under war pressure has been made peculiarly satisfactory in the period, will probably continue to be more friendly than it was in pre-war years. In this crisis capital has become far more sympathetic with the hardships and limitations of labor, and labor in turn has become far more intelligent and discriminating regarding the conditions which attend capital. The labor-union is receiving wiser leadership. That all difficulties in this field have passed away, or are speedily to be eliminated, would be a grossly unjust interpretation, but it is fair to say that the outlook for terms of permanent peace between these two vast forces of humanity is far more promising than it has been for a generation. In all this debate, moreover, armed or unarmed, we are to see a lessened accent on the merely financial and materialistic side of business and an increase of emphasis on the ethical and human side. In fact, a general sense of the unity of all the forces and interests of mankind—a lack of which was one of the hard and dark marks of the last century—is to come to prevail.

The gain which the cause of labor has made during the war, in the consciousness of its own power, and also in a worthy sense of self-respect, will be still further enhanced. Labor will occupy a place yet more compelling over capital and in the general community. In passing it may be said that this enlargement of labor's faculty and function lays on the community a tremendous duty and right of the education of those who at times seem to aspire to become, or may become, its masters.

To one other field I must turn, and it is a field in which my feet are perhaps a little bit less insecure than on any other. I refer to the future of education.

It is evident that the flood-tide of education which arose soon after the close of the Civil War is still to go sweeping on. Its force remains unabated, its volume undiminished, and its height and breadth unlessened. The hunger for education among all Americans, both old and new, seems to have the force of an undying instinct, reënforced by the imperatives of a Puritan conscience. The appetite is recognized in the increasing annual budgets, of public school boards, of colleges, and of all diverse educational agencies. "Americanization" schools form one unique type and illustration of the means used for satisfying the ever-unsatisfied craving. Education, and more and more of it, will be a mark of the next decades. It will prove to be the one great integrating power in our diverse American life. Though not a unit itself, it will tend to create unities.

Education, moreover, will take on forms of vast variety and diversity. Differentiation will be as truly its mark as integration. The variety will be based on the needs of individual children and races so far as these needs can be appreciated by the leaders of the community. These needs will be interpreted in terms personal, and especially in terms of the probable future of American youths. Children whose intellects give little or no response to the stimuli of knowledge after the age of thirteen, but whose wills are interested in doing things, should have, and will have, a different educational course offered to them than that course which is proposed for children whose intellects develop normally with each passing year. Children whose futures are apparently to be commercial or industrial will have, and many should have, an education from the age of thirteen to eighteen unlike that of the boy whose education will be continued up to the age of twenty-four. But be it quickly added that in such early determination of career lies a peril. For many boys and girls do not wake up or find themselves before the age of sixteen. The child may finally eventuate into an early manhood or womanhood which is quite unlike the character which he seemed to possess in his sleepy, changeful, tempestuous, adolescent period. As Lord Bryce has lately said (*Cambridge Essays on Education*,

p. x), "The . . . problem is to find the finest minds among the children of the country and bring them by adequate training to the highest efficiency." The determination of a youth's future should be put off as long as is consistent with keeping that youth interested in his tasks. In this differentiation occupational education will have an enlarging place. Yet be it emphasized that this place may easily become too large. For it is ever to be borne in mind that there is a vast difference between education educative and education occupative.

At the other end of this great subject and force we are to see a vast enrichment. Professional education is to become the object of unexampled improvement. Professional schools, which have since the Civil War been revolutionized in method and somewhat in content of study, are still to be made the object of further strengthening. The chief question concerning them is what degree of improvement is the community willing to pay for —to pay for in dollars, and not in dollars only, but also in higher recognition and appreciation. Theological education is now in a state of flux and flow, and largely by reason of the mixed condition found in the churches. Legal education is to adopt in the large number of its schools standards of admission which now are found in only two or three schools of the whole country, namely, a Bachelor's degree. Their course of study itself is to be made more intellectually remunerative and compelling. Schools of medicine in particular, mighty as is the improvement secured in a generation, are to become agencies of deeper research, of more thorough prophylactic emphasis and of truer interpretation and application of medical facts to the conditions of public health.

We are, further, to find an increase of emphasis on the advantage of the education of women, strong as that emphasis now is. This increase of emphasis will arise from the enlargement of the whole field of professional and other service of women. All professional schools will finally admit them as students. The experience of the recent past gives no ground for fear that the function of the home will be narrowed or made more superficial. We can securely depend on the value of the primitive instincts.

It is my judgment also that the American college system will on the whole remain intact. Covering the four years between the ages of eighteen and twenty-two, or seventeen and twenty-one, it has for the individual youth a sound psychological foundation and significance. The beginning of this quartette of years is too early for the undertaking of professional studies. Of course, the four years will in some colleges be cut down to three by means of continuous sessions, or through the doing of extra work by students; but the system has become so fixed that change will not be made general. The mind of the youth is not sufficiently mature, nor the heart sufficiently firm, nor the will sufficiently strong, to shoulder medical or other pre-professional responsibilities. Education should be built like the geometrical pyramid—not the Egyptian pyramid, a sepulchre for beings that once lived—broad at the base, and by successive, gradual, and broad steps coming to its outlooking, even if narrow, apex. Aside, too, from preparation for the professional school, which the college education gives, and aside from psychological fitness, which nature demands, the college will remain a school of discipline, for gentlemanly living and for large citizenship.

It should also be said that both types of the higher education will persist, the privately endowed and the publicly supported. The elimination of either would be among the greatest of all disasters. Each system can give an educational service which the other cannot.

In all grades of education the physical side will receive increased emphasis. The war has proved that the bodies of our boys and of our men are far less efficient and healthy than they ought to be. The schools and the colleges will give more heed to medical supervision. With this supervision will be united more adequate facilities for the promotion of health and the increase of strength through physical exercise. In some schools and colleges this exercise will take the form of military drill and tactics. It will not be saturated with the war spirit. It will be conditioned by a sense of obedience that the American-born young man has lacked. It will promote an appreciation of courtesy and of respect which also has been lacking. It should be made free from the evils which belong to a universal military training. The present is no place to discuss details of such a system, but such a system as a part of public healthfulness and of individual development should be so adjusted as to lift up the great ends of living, and to increase the force for gaining these ends. It shall not only promote the survival of the physically fit, but it shall also increase the number of the fit.

For education, both of the lower grades and of the highest schools, will come to exist less and less for itself as an end, and more and more as a means for the elevation and development of the supreme object—man himself. Education will be carried on, not for knowledge or for learning or for scholarship primarily, precious as these results or forces are; but rather for life, for life richer in content, broader in relation, more intense in affections, wiser in judgment, more vigorous in self-control, more sympathetic with all, embodying the reverence of the Hebrew, and a sense of the beauty of the Greek, civilization. The more abundant life shall be and will be its goal.

As I read what I have written I find, almost to my surprise, that the prevailing or originating idea of these paragraphs is found in one word—Freedom. It is freedom which characterizes the enlarged or changed headships in the family. To freedom the Church is indebted for its increasing variety of beliefs and of the wider application of its forces. The change of emphasis in governmental relations has arisen under a freer condition of men's minds and of a greater willingness to alter forms and formulas. Business finds its enlargement in theory and in practice through the same great force. Above every other force, too, education discovers in freedom both its end, its fullest content, its wisest method, its best condition, and, in no small degree, its strongest power.

IX

RULING IDEAS IN AMERICAN SOCIETY *

THE American mind is confused; the American heart congested; and American society, composed alike of intellectual and emotional elements, is both congested and confused. Principles, the original foundations on which men base thinking, are lacking. Standards of conduct, types to which all may conform, are also wanting. The issues are many—issues political, educational, religious, industrial, social, national, international. These manifold issues are complex, and therefore perplexing to the intellect and disturbing to the moral nature. The causes of the number and diversity of issues are as numerous and diverse as are the issues themselves, and the issues are quite as involved and unrelated as are the consequent movements and forces. Of course it is a commonplace to say that the American condition is not unique. Alas! it is not. It belongs to all states and nations, even to Cathay and India.

Yet notwithstanding these complexities and perplexities, I am selecting certain elements or conditions in American society, which I am naming

* January, 1925.

ruling ideas, for interpretation. I venture to say that, though many ideas and emotions do seem to be more or less dominant, and that though these ideas and emotions may differ in value or force at different epochs, yet I believe that those which I shall discuss possess, at the present hour, peculiar potency, and hold relationships, broad and deep and high.

An idea which is moving in American society is the idea that America is sufficient unto herself. She is not, indeed, *contra mundum*. Why should she be? She is not against the world any more than the world is against her. Neither antagonism is quite worthy. For she does feel that she can get on without the world, and the world is getting on without her. What is Hecuba to her? What is she to Hecuba? She is, in her present condition, not unlike ancient Thebes, charged with caring only for her own interests, unloving and unloved. Walter Hines Page, in his great *Letters,* writes of the lack of "foreign consciousness" in us Americans. He notes "our isolation." [1] The phrases are apt. They are almost as interpretative as applied to present conditions (in which American banks hold half of the gold of the world) as they were in the dark days when Walter Page first used them. The idea is, indeed, Chauvinistic. It might be charged that the idea is a form of selfishness. But perhaps it is less a form of absolute selfishness

[1] *Life and Letters of Walter Hines Page,* Vol. II, p. 218, and other references.

than of moral indifference and intellectual unconsciousness. It is an example of national provincialism, or of provincial nationalism. Yet it may be noted that such a condition is born rather more of the head than of the heart. The American heart is very tender towards the world's sufferings and the world's woes. Her Near East relief funds, her help for starving villages in Russia and for German children, her outpouring of millions of dollars to the Tokio and Yokohama sufferers, are important examples of her efficient sympathies. Yet if the American heart is responsive to appeals for the needy, the American head is rather ignorant. The American head is ignorant of the world, and ignorance here and now, as ever and everywhere, is the mother of indifference to the world as a fact. In a long and broad historic survey it might be easy to show that such nationalistic interpretations are not unique. Did not such nationalisms show themselves as early as the contests between the Romans and the Britons? Is not megalomania the present mark of the whole world as well as of each individual nation? At its heart such self-centering represents ardent and earnest patriotism. At its worst it is the incarnation of narrow, unhuman, anti-human selfishness or selfwardness. It cries, "My country, right," "My country, wrong," but, whether right or wrong, always "My country!"

It may be added that such patriotic intensity of national narrowness has also its good side. For it does represent an unwillingness of the American people to become mixed up with the internal organizations of other governments and of other peoples. With their parliamentary struggles, with their class antagonisms, with their popular or personal oppositions, with their executive or administrative campaigns for supremacy in leadership, America wishes to have nothing to do. She thinks of herself as a neighbor who, in order to be really neighborly in certain relations, must seem to be unneighborly in other important respects. She wishes to avoid Washington's "entanglements" quite as much in order not to do harm to others as to avoid doing harm to herself.

Of course such an interpretation does not belong equally to all classes of American society, and it does not belong equally to the same class at all times. It shifts indeed from class to class, from age to age, like loose cargo in a ship on tossing seas. At the present writing, in the midst of a national presidential campaign, it belongs to the Republican more than to the Democratic party. The American Republican candidate is declaring for American standards, for American political ideas, for the needlessness of the importing of world goods, either intellectual or industrial or political. He declares for "the American brand." The declarations are a form of the application of the Monroe Doctrine by and to the Northern American continent. In general, the foreign *un*consciousness is a special mark of the great middle class. To this estate the doctrine is a primary belief or atmosphere. The belief is sown with the seed-wheat of the prairies in each spring-tide, and is reaped, without being completely cut down, in the harvest fields of every autumn. It is a prevailing subject of talk also among the directors of banks and trust companies. Neither is it forgotten by the managers of cotton and woolen factories, or of steel and tube mills and of blast furnaces. The so-called lower classes are also deeply touched by it. For these classes are largely composed of recently naturalized citizens, who claim that America is for the new Americans. Their citizenship stands for the well-filled dinner-pail and for regular and fat pay-envelopes. Such material symbols represent, too, the beginning and increasing affection for the new land of their adoption, and by a lessened sense of obligation to the old lands whence they have come. For the foreigner in America soon ceases to be a foreigner to himself.

The class, however, which is the more free from this conception of American self-sufficingness is that small body which would be called the intellectual class. This class is small in America, as in every country. But it has a world vision, a world sympathy, an altruism of the mind and will as well as of the heart. Undoubtedly no small share of this relatively small body will be found among the teachers of the American college and university. For the majority of these men and women have received at least a part of their advanced education abroad, and do continue, even after decades, to think with the international mind and to feel with the international heart. But even if they have not known Oxford, or the Sorbonne, or Leipzig, they yet belong to the thoughtful, or thinking class. They have a world vision, a world interpretation. Narrowness, too, is less prevailing among the religious class than among those who stand outside the Churches. For the cause of foreign missions, beginning in American colleges somewhat more than a century ago—at Williams College and Andover Theological Seminary—has given to the less formal intellectual body a conception of the world as a human brotherhood. This conception, of course, has its origin in the recognition of the Universal Fatherhood of God. Religion, as embodied in the Christian faith, is a most educative force, for the individual and for the community, in a sense of world relations.

This narrow self-sufficiency is, at the present hour, manifesting itself in at least two significant forms. One form is the tendency of the people to limit, and to limit comprehensively and sharply, the number of immigrants whom they are willing to admit within their borders. No longer is America able to regard herself as the refuge of the politically oppressed, or the haven of the industrially enslaved, or the granary and treasury for the personally impoverished. The present Federal laws, recently made more strict, declare that only a certain number of the citizens of any nation—and this number determined by close figuring on the basis of those of the particular nation concerned who were already citizens in the year 1890—can be received.[2]

[2] The Act of Congress, proclaimed by the President on June 30, 1924, declares: "The annual quota of any nationality shall be two per centum of the number of foreign-born individuals of such nationality resident in continental United States as determined by the United States census of 1890, but the minimum quota of any nationality shall be 100."—Sec. 11(a).

"For the purposes of this Act nationality shall be determined by country of birth."—Sec. 12(a).

The present annual immigration quotas are as follows.—

Country.	Quota	Country.	Quota
*Afghanistan	100	Italy (including Dodekanesia, etc.)	3,845
Albania	100	*Japan	100
Andorra	100	Latvia	142
Arabian Peninsula	100	Liberia	100
Armenia	124	Liechtenstein	100
Australia	121	Lithuania	344
Austria	785	Luxemburg	100
Belgium	512	Monaco	100
*Bhutan	100	Morocco	100
Bulgaria	100	*Muscat (Oman)	100
Cameroon (British)	100	Nauru	100
Cameroon (French)	100	*Nepal	100
*China	100	Netherlands	1,648
Czechoslovakia	3,073	*New Guinea, etc.	100
Danzig, Free City of	228	New Zealand	100
Denmark	2,789	Norway	6,453
Egypt	100	Palestine	100
Esthonia	124	Persia	100
Ethiopia (Abyssinia)	100	Poland	5,982
Finland	471	Portugal	503
France	3,954	Ruanda, Urundi	100
Germany	51,227	Rumania	603
Great Britain and Northern Ireland	34,007	Russia, European and Asiatic	2,248
Greece	100	Samoa, Western	100
Hungary	473	San Marino	100
Iceland	100	*Siam	100
*India	100	South Africa, Union of	100
Iraq (Mesopotamia)	100	South-West Africa	100
Irish Free State	28,567		

"America for the Americans" is the slogan. The fair places of the new world, it is declared, shall not be degraded to the base levels of the slums of the old. Berkeley's vision is blurred. For the forthcoming three years only 2 per cent. of the number of foreign born of each nationality of the year 1890 can be admitted. (There are, however, extra quota provisions for wives and children.) On this basis only one hundred and sixty thousand can be admitted each year. After July 1, 1927, the quota is limited to one hundred and fifty thousand, distributed among nationalities according to the national origins of the whole population. The racial significance of this law is seen in such a fact as that of the present population of New York City: Of some seven millions, two millions were born out of the United States, and another two millions are children of the foreign born. These four millions represent more than a half of the entire population. New York is indeed a cross-section of all Europe. It is a microscopic

Country.	Quota	Country.	Quota
Spain	131	Togoland (British)	100
Sweden	9,561	Togoland (French)	100
Switzerland	2,081	Turkey	100
Syria and The Lebanon	100	*Yap, etc.	100
Tanganyika	100	Yugoslavia	671

For each of the countries indicated by an asterisk is established a nominal quota according to the minimum fixed by law. These nominal quotas, as in the case of all quotas hereby established, are available only for persons born within the respective countries who are eligible to citizenship in the United States and admissible under the immigration laws of the United States.—*Foreign Affairs*, Vol. III, No. 1, p. 111.

world, in itself indeed not so microscopic. In New York alone there are no less than one hundred and eighty newspapers published in foreign languages, and there are no less than six hundred social and national organizations. In the whole United States there are no less than a thousand foreign journals. If America is not a foreign country, the great American cities are foreign cities.

On the better side, however, this law is to be interpreted as a measure of national and of domestic self-defence. On the worst and narrowest side, it must be recognized as a method of the labor unions for maintaining their class integrity, and for keeping up wages through lessening the number of those who may receive wages, basing their thought, in part unconsciously, on the old theory of the labor fund. On the best side, indeed, the law stands for national integrity, national individuality, national unity, national self-protection.

A second form of the manifestation of national self-sufficiency is found in what is commonly known as the Ku Klux Klan, the "K.K.K." This society is a vestige, in cabalistic name and method, of the Ku Klux of the Southern States in the years following the Civil War. To this movement or society Mr. S. K. Ratcliffe has referred in fitting terms in an article on "Spiritual Conditions in United States," published in the July number of this Journal. In the Southern States, and in those disastrous years, the ignorant negroes had come into the control of the government of the several reconstructed States. This control originated in, and was supported by, the intense Republican Federal Government. The white citizens of those States resorted to violence to frighten and to overthrow the ignorant, and many would add the corrupt, negro domination. Violence in many cases was triumphant. The negro abandoned his civil rights to save his property, his limbs, his life. Of course the white citizen, though recognizing its unlawfulness, defended its practice. He has associates, too, who still defend themselves under an interpretation of Cicero's dictum of the silence of the laws in time of war. The present movement has made use of the mysterious, terrifying practice of the post-Civil War years. Its members also have adopted the principles of the Know Nothing movement of the decade before the outbreak of the Civil War, and of the American Protective Association (A.P.A.) of the decade following that struggle. The principles of these two somewhat diverse movements were, however, quite identical. The principles were the necessity of maintaining American national integrity, honor, prestige, and of preserving the purity of the American life by the exclusion of, or at least by diminishing the influence of, foreigners. The modern K.K.K. directs its power against three classes—the Negro, the Roman Catholic, and the Jew. It is a movement social, racial, and religious. A white America and a Protestant America are the two foci of the new Chauvinistic ellipse. The power of this modern movement is still obscure. For the first time, as a general organization, its strength will be known, or at least intimated, in the forthcoming Federal election. But in States as remote and as unlike as Maine and Texas, it has become one of the more powerful of political forces. It adjusts itself to local conditions. In Maine, for instance, it is directed against the Roman Catholic, and in the Southern States against the negro. Though in Texas, be it added, there is a Roman Catholic element provided by France in the last decades.

Concerning the causes, transient or permanent, of the current doctrine of the self-sufficiency of America to herself, I content myself with pointing out three as peculiarly significant and dominant: first, historical antagonisms; second, geographical isolation; and third, industrial, commercial, and financial power. The historical antagonisms, be it at once confessed, are largely directed towards a country which some of us like to think of, and to love, as our Mother Country. Yet it is also to be said that America, and many American institutions, had their origin as a protest against the government and certain practices of that country. The Pilgrim movement was a protest. The Puritan movement was a protest. The American Revolution of 1775-83 was a protest. The war of 1812 was a protest. Many of the diplomatic movements of the Civil War were nothing less than protests. The behavior of the American government in the Venezuela affair—a rather ruthless and, some would add, purposely ruthless, behavior—was a protest. The "ancient grudge," though becoming more ancient and becoming less and less of a grudge, is still somewhat remembered and felt.

Furthermore, and secondly, America is remote in space from the world's capitals and the world's movements. She is outside of the historic tendencies and currents. She is divided from Europe by an ocean several times bigger than the European Mediterranean. The British Commonwealth of Nations—what has America to correspond to such a democratic imperialism or imperialistic democracy, bound together by its red, globe-encircling cords! To the world, America might be interpreted as a foreign country.

Third, is it not to be recognized that, above most countries, America is self-sufficing in all material conditions and forces? Do not her latitudes and longitudes, her soils and mines, her coasts and plains, her variety of seasons, inevitably contribute to such a conclusion? Is there any people less dependent upon foreign aid for a good living? Does not, furthermore, her history confirm the teaching of her geography and geology? Is it not, indeed, to be recognized that America has really succeeded in her industrial, commercial, and financial concerns far more greatly than her enemies feared or than her friends and citizens dared to hope? In her heart of hearts has America not the right to believe that she, in a narrow and lower sense, is self-sufficient? Do not these three causes, historical, geographical, material, help somewhat to explain America's self-sufficingness? They do not, indeed, justify it, but they do give some intimation of the causes of the fact and of the prevalence of the consequent belief.

Before I pass on to another of the ruling ideas of American society, I wish to add a paragraph regarding the application of the American conception of self-sufficiency to the present hour. For there is an application to the element of time, as well as to the organized State or unorganized community. The American believes in the *now,* in the *eternal now.* He thinks that the now is to be everlasting. Yesterday was, and yesterday has ceased to be. History is not. Tomorrow has not dawned, and its sun, as Dr. Thomas Arnold might intimate, may never rise. Today is, and today alone is. Tomorrow has not come: in fact it never does. The American conjugates life's verb in the present tense. In a bad sense, such a temporal and timely interpretation creates narrowness of vision, limitation of interest, intellectual and emotional, provincialism of service. But in its higher sense such an interpretation does minister to directness of aim, to intensity of endeavor, and to an ascending, even if a narrowing, achievement. Mountain-peaks grow smaller as they go higher.

A second ruling idea is what I shall call by the awkward name of direct, political, executive action. This method of practice is at once to be discriminated, first, from control by the mob, and, secondly, from direction by legislation. The control by the mob is, of course, less important and far less serious. For, despite such outbreaks as occurred in Herrin, Illinois, over labor troubles last year, and in such riots as suddenly burst forth in negro lynchings, the mob in American society is an anomaly, and also a diminishing force. At once it can be eliminated from the present discussion. In his article in the July (1924) number of The *Hibbert Journal* Mr. Ratcliffe writes of "the instinctive resort to mob violence."[3] The Americans, be it at once said, do resort to mob violence, but the resort, I do firmly believe, is not instinctive. It is sporadic, it is far from being an instinct, and the instances of such violence are becoming more and more exceptional. But, secondly, direct, political, executive action, as opposed to government through legislation, is a growing characteristic, and a political force becoming more formative. Of the fact there is no doubt. The fact receives reiterated interpretations in leading American journals, forms one of the stated topics of talk among intelligent citizens, and was indeed made the subject of an address in a leading university at its commencement a year ago by the Secretary of War. Of course this move-

[3] Page 639.

ment is only a part of a similar world movement. Fascism is possibly its most outstanding token. Spain has been touched, of course, by the current tendency. Bolshevism represents its worst development. Gossamer threads of thought and of practice bind together all nations. Herein America is not a foreign country.

The reasons for the decline of legislation and the increase of direct executive power are diverse, complex, and perhaps cannot be made thoroughly satisfactory in any interpretation addressed to the thoughtful. Among these causes may be noted, first, that the passing of many laws—and the laws passed at any annual or biennial session of the State legislatures of the forty-eight States and by the Federal Congress are literally to be numbered by the thousands—is a cause of the decline of respect for all law. Laws are like the currency— the more one has the less is the value. A second cause undoubtedly lies in the current American disobedience to all laws. Disobedience to laws springs out of disrespect for law, and, of course, it is equally true that disrespect for law is an evil outgrowth of disobedience to laws. Every American is, in a sense, a declaration of independence. A third cause is found in the character of the lawmakers themselves. This character fails to embody the best elements of American society. These best elements represent thoughtfulness, largeness of mind, greatness of heart, comprehensiveness in far-off vision, considerateness of the deepest and permanent welfare of all the people. Most legislators are selected on a petty, narrow, partisan basis. They are thus selected either as a reward for service already given to the party, or as an opportunity for future service to the party, or as the expression of a hope of service yet to be rendered.

On such bases poverty and ineffectiveness of legislative service is inevitable. The laws made by such law-makers cannot, of course, command either obedience or respect.

Yet these three causes which I name are perhaps quite as much symptoms as creative forces. For behind them lies, in my judgment, a power which in turn is their cause, a power which makes direct, political, executive action a ruling idea. That power is the power of individualism. Individualism, excessive individuality, placed in the White House, seated in the governor's chair of the single Commonwealth, is bound to make itself a controlling fact and factor in governmental affairs. Of course there are exceptions, numerous ones; but, as a practice, strong personalities of excessive individualism are put into the highest executive offices. Such was the personality of Lincoln, though the nobility of the personality was guided and characterized by calm judgment and by intellectual and emotional altruism. Such a personality was Cleveland, such was Roosevelt, and such was Woodrow Wilson. The characteristic, too, is not remote from the governors of individual Commonwealths and from the mayors of the great cities. For better or for worse, the legislators federal, or of the individual Commonwealth or municipality, are more or less controlled, or forcefully influenced, by the executive. Such executive masters can promote or delay or alter legislation. Such masters can act, and do act, without legislation. Such masters have been charged, in most serious and complex circumstances of even an international character, in recent years, as acting in apparent disobedinece to laws and to international understandings and conventions. Exceptions to this interpretation of controlling masterfulness are, as I have intimated, not lacking. Exceptions relate to the placing in executive positions of intellectual weaklings and of volitional passivities. But the exceptions are fundamentally no exceptions to the power of direct, executive action. For such passive personalities are usually put into their office by a clique, by a steering committee, by a machine, by a gang, who rule their appointees or nominees for their selfish, direct, official, and personal purposes.

The reception given to the instances of and to the practice of direct, political, executive action, and to the movement out of which such acts spring, by the whole body of people is most significant. The reception given by the whole body of the people, be it at once affirmed, in the by and large, is favorable. The people as a whole approve such power and commend its use. The people like swiftness. Legislation is slow. Action is swift. Legislation is a written document, a "scrap of paper." Action is a doing, and the people like to see, to hear, to feel doing, and they also like to do. Legislation is more statical than dynamic. Action is more dynamic than statical. The American people prefer to be dynamic. They like to go, even if they do not know whither they go. The forces have got ahead of the intellectual judgment to guide those forces unto a proper goal. The will has become superior to the intellect.

Of course the more thoughtful classes of American society are not sympathetic with the prevailing decline of the law-making movement, or with the increase of the law-breaking spirit, or with the rise of the direct, executive power. Their vision is still centered upon the Congressional end of Pennsylvania Avenue and not upon the White House. They recognize that, historically, the direct, political, executive action leads, under many conditions, to dictatorships. Yet their serious thoughtfulness seldom solidifies itself into Cassandra-like prophecies. The forces of order, as of the integrity of the family, of the sacredness of property, of the conservatism of the Church, of the respect paid to the Supreme Court, the general firmness of the several structures that constitute government, the thoughtful classes still believe will prove to be sufficient, as they have in the past proved to be sufficient, to save the State from the despotism of a Cæsar or the devastations of a Napoleon. It is still true, as de Tocqueville wrote three-quarters of a century ago:

"Democratic governments may become violent, and even cruel, at certain periods of extreme effervescence or of great danger; but these crises will be rare and brief. When I consider the petty passions of our contemporaries, the mildness of their manners, the extent of their education, the purity of their religion, the gentleness of their morality, their regular and industrious habits, and the restraint which they almost all observe in their vices no less than in their virtues, I have no fear that they will meet with tyrants in their rulers, but rather with guardians." [4]

The third ruling idea relates to religion. Religion in turn connotes the Christian religion, and this faith is, by common consent, made to stand for the Protestant type. The Protestant faith still recognizes its right, and perhaps its duty, of still protesting. It therefore naturally divides itself into scores of faiths. Of these many and diverse types the different Churches are the normal exponent and organ. The ordinary Protestant thinks quite as devotedly of his Church as of his creed. For the Church is a definite, formal, visible existence, easy to realize, to thought, feeling, conscience, will. The faith or the creed in turn calls for a thinking which is a more difficult task for

[4] *Democracy in America*, by Alexis de Tocqueville, Vol. II, p. 391.

the mind to undertake or to understand. The American people accept religion as a form of the idealism to which they are consciously or unconsciously devoted. Its Churches are coming to be divided into the two types of the Liberal and the Conservative. At present the division is almost as marked as was the division of a hundred years ago in the Congregational body of New England, which resulted in the great historic Unitarian movement and organization. Of this movement Harvard College was, for a generation, the intellectual exponent, Channing the apostle, and Emerson the transcendental prophet. At the present moment the Conservative is known as fundamentalist—a distinction of somewhat obscure origin, and yet perhaps supposed to stand for the faith delivered once for all to the saints. The Liberal party still retains, and delights to retain, its old name. This division runs through all the Churches, but at present belongs more deeply and aggressively to the Baptist and the Presbyterian. The orthodox Congregational Church fought out a similar issue forty years ago, in which, as is usual, the freedom of the Liberal wing won. Consideration has been given to dividing these two commanding Churches, the Baptist and the Presbyterian, upon the great lines of conservatism and liberalism. In fact, a leading Baptist clergyman of the Liberal type said to me recently, "We may come over and join you Congregationalists." But the danger of such a split, or of such a union, lessens. For, on the whole, the Liberal wing is winning in the battle of the creeds. It is, moreover, generally recognized that it is wise for the Baptists to remain Baptists and for the Presbyterians to remain Presbyterians, and to maintain their faiths in their own fields and under their own flags. Ecclesiastical transfers do not make for the progress of the Divine Kingdom.

In the United States, as in most parts of the world, the permanent interest of the Churches is directed, in thought, discussion, and decision, towards the three points: First, of freedom in the interpretation of the Bible; secondly, freedom in the interpretation and validity of the ecumenical creeds; and thirdly, with a lessening value, freedom in the use of Sunday as a day of rest and of worship. To neither side of this threefold division does American Christianity have special contributions to offer. English thought and German have preceded American in this whole domain. There is, however, a fourth part of this field to which anxious discussion is at present given. It is the field of the ministry. The number of properly qualified candidates for the sacred calling diminishes at an alarming rate, and the candidates themselves, in point of general and special abilities, become apparently less worthy. One half of the graduates of the leading colleges now enters business. The other half is divided up among those choosing the law, medicine, teaching, engineering, editorship, leaving a bare modicum for the priesthood. To consider the causes for this change would just now carry one too far afield. It may be added, however, that the same scarcity of proper candidates for the Roman Catholic priesthood also is creating a sense of anxiety among the leaders of that historic Church.

In any interpretation of the place of religion in American society emerges the movement known as Christian Science. Christian Science is, like all religions, a form of idealism. Its very idealism is, of course, one cause, perhaps the chief cause, of the appeal which it makes to the rank and file of the American people. Its idealism, too, constitutes the basis of the appeal which it makes to the intellectual classes. Its growth has been tremendous. This growth, like its origin, has been fostered, at least negatively, by what may be called, for want of a better term, the materialism, or the spiritual emptiness, of the typical Protestant Church. The typical Protestant Church has lacked, and still lacks, a spiritual accent and atmosphere. That enlargement of thought, that far-off vision, that comfort which is cried for in harrowing disappointments and in smiting and sinking griefs, that uplift of the soul, which worshipers wish to find in their Church service and do not find, have turned thousands and tens of thousands to the doors of the Christian Science temples. The present methods of and content of the Protestant Church represent a bad religious psychology. Akin to this fact is also the lack of the presentation of the mystical element in the Christian life. The Protestant faith has emphasized absolute intellectual clearness as it ought. But with this emphasis it has forgotten the atmospheres, psychological and philosophical. It has not given a proper place to the feelings. The signs of the consequent power of the Christian Science movement are not lacking. It builds churches which, often supporting the Moslem dome, have the magnificence of many Catholic cathedrals. The loyalty of its worshipers at its Sunday and mid-week service may well put to shame the Episcopal, the Congregational, and other communions. It publishes a daily journal of unique worth: The *Monitor* is a sort of monthly review, in news and interpretation, of the current affairs of the world. Whether the movement, as a movement, has come to its highest crest and will decline, or whether it will mount yet higher, is a question which the thoughtful discuss and upon which there is no assured verdict. On the whole I should judge, and with humility of spirit, that the specific and fundamental truths of the faith will be taken over by the more historic Churches. Therefore, as a specific movement, it will decline. Such has been the history of the many preceding movements of organized Christianity. The Free-will Baptist Church and the Quaker communion are historic illustrations.

The religion of America, as I have intimated, is primarily Protestant. Towards the enlarging freedom of its Churches, the Roman Catholic Church bears itself in splendid isolation and in a silence almost unbroken. That faith goes on with its undying traditions, unreasoning beliefs, quiet propaganda, supporting its schools and convents, founding universities in metropolitan districts from the Atlantic to the Pacific—having its center and source of direction far over the seas. It is easy, however, and natural to imagine its hierarchy as watching the movements and swiftly changing atmospheres of Protestant Christianity with keenest emotions. Freedom of religious thought tending to theological latitudinarianism, latitudinarianism leading to indifference to the Christian faith, indifference leading to irreverence, irreverence to agnosticism, agnosticism to atheism, and both agnosticism and atheism leading to contempt of standards of conduct, and this contempt to immoral and disintegrating practice—such may easily be pictured as the logical decline and inevitable fall, in the Catholic mind, of the Protestant faith and order. Whatever of regret may attend such lapses, the Catholic mind cannot but reason that they are the necessary result of the acceptance of Protestant assumptions, axioms, creeds, and principles.

It would be at once vain and unbecoming in me even to intimate what the immediate future holds for American Protestant Christianity. But yet it may not be altogether unfitting to say that the characteristic freedom which may become, to some, footfalls, may also lead others to the foothills, and thus and thence to the mountain-peaks of the Christian faith. This freedom of belief in matters religious is as great, as genuine, and as inevitable as the freedom of belief and practice in matters political. In this very freedom, and in the consequent adaptability of belief to organization, and of organization to environment, lies hopefulness of the survival of the truest and of the best, and gives ground for trust in unending progress.

Closely associated, in both history and logic, with religion in the United States is the cause of education. For the American people are as a body devoted to education, and never have they been so devoted as at the present time. The devotion of each year seems to gather up the devotions of the preceding times, and to this devotion are made rich and positive additions. This devotion is well indicated by the increased cost of education. In the last thirty years the cost has increased some sixfold, and now amounts, in all grades from the kindergarten to the university, each year, to more than two billions of dollars. Of course a part of this cost is to be attributed to the lessening value of the purchasing power of the dollar. But there are other causes, yet more important, which do give evidence of the interest of the people in the great movement. Students have increased many-fold, and in no part in a larger proportion than in the colleges and universities. The number at present approaches a million. Colleges are now enrolling as many students in their Freshman class as, thirty years ago, were enrolled in all their classes. The field of education has greatly enlarged, not only in respect to the so-called fundamentals, but also through the addition of more courses in the sciences, in language (except Greek), in history, in psychology and philosophy, in economics and sociology, and in all that makes up vocational training. The people have demanded buildings more completely furnished for the safety, for the health, and for the happiness of all students. They have more than doubled the salaries of teachers, and also have, in many States, established a pension system for teachers on their retirement. Through the public schools, too, the community is functioning in respect to societies and organizations for social betterment, for the Americanization of the foreign-born, and for a better appreciation of civic duty. Continuation schools and classes are established, the movement for adult education is well begun. The people are interpreting the function of education in the broadest possible way for the making of human betterment, as they also have given similar interpretation to the function of the civil government.

At times the people give evidence for believing that they are not getting the results they desire, and ought to get, for the increased expenditure and for the enlargement of educational function.

For they have come to recognize that the vocational teaching given in the schools has, on the whole, been a failure. They have come to see, as President Pritchett, of the Carnegie Foundation for the Advancement of Teaching, has pointed out:

"The public school makes its greatest contribution to training in the crafts when it teaches boys and girls in the elementary school to do such work there as will give them the discipline of mind and the accuracy of knowledge necessary to enter a skilled craft. The greatest service the elementary school can do for the boy who wants to be a carpenter, or a mason, or a machinist, or an electrician, or a printer, or a glazier, will not be accomplished by trying to teach him something about any of these skilled trades. It will do the greatest possible service for him if it sees to it that he knows the English language well . . . that he has acquired in the process of his elementary education that thoroughness of knowledge in these simple subjects and that ability to turn his mind to one problem or another which will qualify him to go into a trade school and to do its work so well that the trade school will not have to teach him English and elementary mathematics. With the best intentions on the part of those who originated these courses, the introduction of vocational training into the high school has in a considerable measure served only to lead men away from those high and honorable vocations which find expression in a sincere and accurate craftsmanship, and to entice them into occupations that are already overcrowded and that play a small rôle in the work of production." [5]

The people have also come to believe that the schools should attempt to give, directly or indirectly, more adequate education in the moral verities and veracities. The Downing Professor at Cambridge said, at the last Harvard Commencement:

"Society is urgently in need of an inner moral reformation, a reawakening within every body politic, including our own Republic, of the nobler emotions, passions, and aspirations of men; and the necessity for this moral rejuvenation is, in many respects, far greater than for increased intellectual dexterity and power. The very future of our civilization rests largely upon the cultivation of higher moral ideals and their general application to the manifold activities of life." [6]

The crime-wave that is sweeping over America, in which youth seems to bear the most significant and horrible part, gives evidence of the truth of

[5] "The Teacher's Responsibility for our Educational Integrity," by Henry S. Pritchett, of the Carnegie Foundation for the Advancement of Teaching, *Eighteenth Annual Report*, 1923, pp. 87-88.
[6] *Journal of Education*, July 10, 1924, p. 50.

the interpretation of the Downing Professor. In half-unconsciousness the people are coming to realize this truth. They are quickened into requiring that the schools shall train the moral character of students. They are demanding that education shall not only educate the girl and boy in making a living, but also in making a life. They wish that education shall promote health of body, sanity of mind, usefulness of the citizen, a respect for and obedience to the laws of man and of nature, but they also demand that it shall aid youth in having regard for the ethical principles and the moral practices that make for the happiness and the betterment of men. George Washington in his "Farewell Address" indicated that, as the institutions of democracy become the more free, it is of greater importance that the education of the people should be made the more adequate. The institutions of America have gone, and are going, to almost the breaking-point of freedom. The people therefore realize it is of the most fundamental importance that the education should be adequate for the whole life, and especially for the moral character of the individual.

There are two other fields in which ideas are at least beginning to rule, to which any just survey of American society requires reference be made, even if briefly.

One of these fields is what may be called the domain of the privileged. In every nation are found the privileged classes. The classes have long existed, and apparently long will continue to exist. Numerous and diverse are the causes which have created, and still create them, which have perpetuated, and will still perpetuate, them. Causes communal, causes individual, causes domestic, causes dynastic, causes commercial, causes financial, causes literary, causes scholastic, have in turn made, and are still making, their contributions to this happy, or unhappy, result. America in three hundred years has built up—like England and France, like Spain and Italy, in a far longer period—its privileged classes. At present the great body of the American electorate has decided, in part consciously, in part at least unconsciously, that the privileged classes shall be wiped out, or, if not wiped out, shall have many of their richest privileges taken away. There is no Reign of Terror, and there is not to be any. There is no fear of the guillotine or of the murdering guns of Moscow. But there is a quiet decision that many of the privileges of the privileged class shall be cut off; and there is a further conviction that many of these privileges ought to be cut off. No small share of these privileges come from inherited wealth. The electorate has decided that wealth shall not be inherited unimpaired. Great wealth, it is argued, belongs quite as much to the community or to the State as to the children and grandchildren of those who have made it. If the good luck of the landholder, or the genius of the industrialist, or the laboriousness of the merchant, have created and nourished great wealth, it is the increase of the number of the people, or the enlargement of their wants, which have caused the amassing of large fortunes. The unearned increment represents no small share of the consummate result. Therefore it is inferred that at least a share of these fortunes shall be ultimately returned to the Commonwealth. It is a form of argumentation used quite as freely and as fittingly in Western Europe as in Eastern America. The ultimate change is made at the death of the creator or possessor of wealth. Therefore the individual American State and the Federal Government have, by the gradual passing of laws in recent years, been determining that a proportion of these large accumulations shall not follow the formerly recognized lines of devolution. The State has declared that a share of these great fortunes shall go back to all the people from whom they were formerly derived. The most significant of all these decisions is found in the Act of the Federal Congress, passed in the year 1924. This Act, taken in connection with similar fiscal legislation, covers taxation by the Federal Government of, first, annual income; second, of the inheritance of property; and third, of gifts. For my present purpose it is enough to say that this Act—consisting of no less than seventy-five thousand words—and the preceding Acts declare that the Government shall take forty per cent. of all inheritances and gifts above ten million dollars, and also forty per cent. of all annual incomes over five hundred thousand dollars. The percentage lessens as the aggregate sums lessen. Gifts, however, to religious, charitable, educational institutions are to an extent exempt. Certain exceptions to the general law, moreover, are allowed. The motives lying behind this system of taxation are not only those which I have already indicated; but also, first, to get income for administering the Government, as administration becomes every month more costly; and, second, to satisfy the public sentiment that it does not make for the public welfare for great fortunes to remain for generations in the possession of a single family. This Act, one may also say in passing, may be interpreted as showing the growth of a distinctly socialistic principle as a moving force in legislation and in life.

This most recent and momentous decision has been received by the American people in excellent spirit. The people as a body have quietly recognized its fitness, and even those who are possessed of large property have not rebelled. In fact, the two great fortunes in America of the last decades have been given back, and are still being given back, to the people. These benefactions, it may be said, enrich not only America but also the world. Mr. Andrew Carnegie gave away, in his life and by his will, not less than ninety per cent. of his fortune, or more than four hundred millions. What proportion Mr. Rockefeller has given, or will bequeath, no one knows, but it is safe to say that this proportion is larger by much than the proportion which governmental death-duties, as now fixed, would represent.

To another idea, less potential, indeed less general, than those I have discussed, I wish as I close to allude. Mr. Ratcliffe in his admirable article, to which I already have made reference, writes of the "incessant experimental character of the people."[7] Interpreting the phrase as referring to the experimenting force or element, it is a most happy term. For the people of America are engaged in a huge political, a huge industrial, a huge educational, a huge social experiment. They, the people of the commonwealth, do not commonly think of themselves as experimentalists. The thoughtful class, however, do know, and feel, that America is a trial, a testing, of tremendously vast human forces, united with equally vast forces of nature. The people go on, day by day, year by year, working and playing with the consistency and the variableness of the stars, confident that all is well, and that all will continue to be well. Only few know that it is all an experiment. The literary class indeed do recognize that to them, and to all, the age is one of experimentation. Likewise know and feel the educated classes. The thoughtful and the reverent also work and think, play and pray, hope and fear, that all will be well, eager to adjust forces, human and natural, to

[7] Page 643.

each other and in proper proportion, by just methods, and determined to direct these forces under some far-off divine event which, even if now unknown, will make for the achieving of the ultimate good. The thoughtless and the irreverent also work and play, likewise unconsciously feeling that out of the turmoil and the welter will emerge finally a happy result. But all classes agree that America is the land of experimentation, and all classes, as one body, are willing to wait for conclusions.

X

WHAT ARE THE TESTS OF A NATION'S CIVILIZATION?*

CAN AMERICA MEET THEM?

THE first test which I name as belonging to a nation is appreciation of its past. That past may embrace centuries; it may cover decades only. But, long or short, a nation which forgets its past, which eliminates the causes, forces, conditions, and results of its past, is failing to respect the riches which belong to it and which it should respect. The nation which comes before the judgment-seat of history with hands empty and with mind and understanding vacant, may not be judged as barbarous, but it cannot justly be called civilized. It has forgotten what Aristotle said to Alexander: "Remember the difference between a Greek and a Barbarian." Capital is defined as the result of past savings. Without capital large commerce is impossible. So likewise civilization is based, in part at least, on the appreciation of the results won in the past of a nation. Of course the law of proportions is to be observed. Ancestor worship may limit and fetter present achieve-

* January, 1929.

ment. In China graveyards are religious altars, but from them comes little power. At the other extreme from China stands Greece. What would be the condition of modern Greece if she had had no appreciation of her Olympia, her Delphi, her Parthenon, her Marathon? What would be her condition if she had forgotten her Homer, her Æschylus, her Plato, her Aristotle?

A second test of a lasting civilization is seen in its power to create and to maintain institutions. An institution is the result of the accumulation and working of human forces. These personal forces represent the control of other forces which are not personal. Humanity is like a great river gathering its waters from many plains and slopes, enlarging its power as its flow lengthens, and finally emptying itself into the all-receiving ocean. Men are born, live for a time in relations large or small, and finally dissolve themselves in the all-receiving tomb. The river was naught and the river becomes naught. But on the banks of the river are built great cities, and out of its waters are drawn forces for use in the manifold agencies of men. These cities, these agencies, represent lasting institutions. They are the permanent institutions for receiving and for perpetuating, as well as for creating, mankind's achievements. Colleges and universities are such institutions, for without them the torch of learning would fall and be extinguished. Banks are such institutions, for they treasure the material results of man's toil, saving these results and transmitting them to the generations following. The individual dies, the institution, educational, financial, composed of individuals, lives. The civil government is such an institution. It represents the orderly and normal process through which and under which men live in prosperity, peace, good-will, and happiness. Dissolve the civil government and anarchy reigns; for anarchy spells not only no government, but also antagonisms, destructions, annihilations. For fifteen hundred years Western civilization was saved, though at times the salvation seemed uncertain and futile, by three institutions—the Empire, the Papacy, and the Universities.

A third test of a permanent civilization is found in the power of men to combine. The unifying of men for any one of several purposes is essential. Combination is one element or force in the process by which institutions are created. If the individual persist in standing alone or single, he perishes, and his works run the severe risk of also perishing with him. If he unite other individuals with himself, or himself with other individuals, and if their successors also call on still other personalities to join them from generation to generation, such unifications represent increasing richness of every resource and give assurance of permanence. Weaknesses are corrected, structural foundations strengthened, personal adjustments made, and personal aptitudes appreciated and utilized.

A fourth test, and one of the more fundamental,

is what I shall call by the general name of altruism. A nation like the individual is to seek to see with the intellectual eye, and to feel and to understand with the emotional and intellectual mind and heart of other nations. In this process there are at least three steps or functions: A nation is first to seek to understand other nations; it is, secondly, to have the mood of tolerance, either active or passive; it is also, thirdly, to try to respect all the rights which belong to other nations. Understanding, forbearance, the sense of duty form this three-corded test. These are indeed the tests of the gentleman. Why should not a nation adopt and use them? Why should not the term the "gentlestate" come to be as common and to possess the great connotations of the gentleman? The nation which affirms that "my position is right" and every other position wrong, is by such an affirmation virtually put outside the circle of civilization. The Bismarcks of the future shall have no place as the heads of civilized states. Long is the process, slow is the progress; but the consummation is certain. The contrast in this respect between the early policy of Spain in dealing with her colonies, and the later policy of Great Britain in dealing with her dependencies, is impressively significant. Spain primarily sought to make her colonies contribute to her wealth and her other power, she alone had rights, they had only duties; and she lost both her colonies and herself. Great Britain has sought to develop her colonies for their own primary worths, both parties had both rights and duties; and they have stood by her side in her supreme crises.

I have written that the test of the lasting civilization of a nation is respect for its past. An identical remark may be made substituting the word future for the word past. If the understanding of the past is concerned with results already won, the future is concerned with results absolutely unknown. But as a nation faces that unknown future, that nation is to prepare for both certainties and uncertainties. It is to develop its material resources. Many of these resources, once used up, cannot be recreated. It is to promote loyalty on the part of its younger citizens; and to these citizens it is to give the best education which the State can afford, or which the citizens can profit by. Education of all kinds, fitted to all sorts and conditions of men, is also to be established and promoted. The nation which thinks only of today may or may not have a good present, but it certainly cannot have a good future.

A sixth test concerns the family. The present condition of the family as an institution of civilized society represents and embodies a long, diverse and historic process. Whatever the early condition and relation of the sexes—promiscuity, polygamy, polyandry—it is clear that monogamy is now recognized among most peoples as the crown of the developing process. Monogamy represents the best method and the most efficient means for the development of the race. It stands for the happiness and well-being of the two constituent partners. It gives the most assured promise for the protection and the development of children. This protection applies to infantile helplessness and to the development of the moral and intellectual condition of youth. Stained by lust, destroyed by divorce, both as a fact and as a symbol, the family becomes a menace to civilization. The abolition of the family, or the elimination of marriage which is the foundation of the family, would result inevitably in the sexual uncertainties or abnormalities which mean social and human anarchy.

There is another test of a lasting civilization—it is in order the seventh—which it is specially difficult to formulate. I shall, however, call it a union of the stable and the flexible in the civil government. The contrast between a government both stable and flexible on the one side, and a government on the other side absolute and fixed, is broad and deep. The contrast, too, between these two types of government and a government anarchistic is no less wide and deep. A government may indeed be stable, absolute and monarchical. It is simply statical. Such a government cannot normally represent or embody the highest and most developing forces of civilization. The government which, too, is anarchistic, is no government at all. It lacks standards. Its forces, be they few or many, are inefficient for securing desirable ends. But the government which is stable, regular, orderly, and which also is capable of change, represents a civil control which has standards, and forces, which can be reckoned with, and which makes adjustments, too, to changing conditions. With the exception of a few periods the government of early Rome, both of the Republic and of the Empire, embodied such a condition. It was at once fixed and fluid. It was both imperial and democratic. It stood for the statute and also for the variable human element. The Roman Empire continued for its centuries because it did embody these two elements. In modern history the British Empire, or the British Commonwealth of Nations, represents most impressively the union of the stable and of the flexible.

An eighth element in this testing process is found in the respect paid to the preservation of the life and of the health of citizens. Of course such a standard is more than obvious, for life is a pre-requisite to all human forces and conditions. If life be taken away, all else that is founded on, or is nourished by, life falls and is extinguished. If no respect is paid to life, no respect is paid to what springs from life. If respect is paid to life, assurance is given of a proper respect for the institutions and agencies which originate in it. Of course, also, a similar interpretation may be applied to the force which nourishes and preserves life, the health of the community and of the individual. A state which defends the life of its citizens, which by all measures and methods, active and passive, seeks to eliminate disease, to promote physical and other strength, to lengthen the span of years allotted to the average citizen, to increase the happiness which ministers to health, and to lessen the miseries which dissipate vigor, such a state meets a primary test of permanent civilization.

Closely associated with the test touching life and health is a further test relative to property. The origin of the institution of individual property is hidden in the prehistoric mists. But whatever may have been that origin, it is clear that, throughout all historic periods, the fact of individual property is found. Apparently the *meum* and the *tuum* is an early, a primary, and a fundamental distinction. The brute has it and exercises it. Early does the human infant show it. To attempt to do away with it is a process shot through and through with all kinds of difficulties. The attempt seems to foreshadow a result of defeat and disaster. Its possession is not, indeed, free from liabilities of many sorts. The duties which it imposes, as well as the rights which it bestows, are never to be denied. The powers which go along with it are great, at times colossal. The risks which it confers are not to be hidden. The passions created in its gaining, or holding, or losing, are intense. Yet, nevertheless, property is a result of civilization. The savage has a conception of it in a low form. As a result of civilization it creates or measures a standard for judging civilization. The material aids in evaluating the non-material.

A further test, comprehensive and fundamental, of a permanent civilization is found in the respect paid to the mind of man. What test could be broader or deeper? Is not the mind, using the term in its most general sense, the outcome of the whole developing process and the crown of the lasting human forces? Is it not the image of God in humanity? Are not its thoughts the highest, its reasonings the most abstruse, its sentiments the noblest, its imaginations the farthest flung, its creations the most divine, its knowings the most comprehensive in time and place? Is it not, therefore, true that the civilization which has its chief treasure in the great minds of the race is thereby proved to be the best, the most lasting, and the highest? This civilization may manifest itself in forms many and diverse. It may and will show itself in creations of the beautiful. It will declare itself in architecture. It will build the Parthenon and medieval cathedrals. It will reveal itself on the canvas and will discover the Venus of Milo and the Hermes in the marble. It will speak out in literature, singing in the poem, interpreting in essay, and teaching in history. It will go to nature, reading the thoughts of the divine creator, weighing the planets, picturing stars that the eye cannot see, interpreting laws of the worlds, finding a universe in a single drop of water:—the mind telescopic, the mind microscopic. Ah, what infinities of knowledge! The mind of man and the civilization of man! Herein lies a supreme test.

As a method and means of disciplining the mind of man, yet a further test is revealed. It is education. Is a nation educated? Does it believe in, and is it loyal to, education? Is the education of its youth dearer than either war or war's victories? As a political body does it promote efficient measures for the maintenance of schools and colleges and universities? Does it give of its revenues to the support and endowment of education in its manifold institutions and diverse agencies? Does it think of itself in terms of its youth, youth which represents the field and the conditions of education? Is the education which it fosters genuine, sincere, fundamental, formative, creative? If such questions can be answered in the affirmative, that nation is so far forth proved to be civilized.

Yet there is a test of civilization yet more supreme. It is the test to be applied not to the known but to the unknown: not to and by the mind of man, but to the mind of God. It lies in the mood or attitude which man holds to the Infinite Father. I use the words God, Infinite Father, in a sense personal. But if one should prefer to write god and infinite father, my argument would still hold. For I have in mind the absolute, the ultimate being, the thing-in-itself, the unknown, the unknowable behind the known. The test applies equally well to the personal or to the impersonal infinite being. What should be the mood or the attitude of man to that being? It may be the mood of indifference. It may be the mood of antagonism and defiance. It may be the mood of reverence, of obedience, of worship. The people to whom the mood of indifference is normal are unresponsive, hard of heart, and hard of mind. The people to whom the mood of antagonism and defiance is normal are the victims of tragic fate. The people to whom the mood of reverence, of obedience, and of worship is normal are the people highest in thought, deepest in emotion, noblest, best, measured by all standards, truly and justly weighed in the balances of infinite justice. Such a people worthily meets the supreme test of a permanent civilization.

Such are some of the tests which I would apply to a civilization—to learn whether it gives promise of lastingness. Each of these tests has, I believe, a certain degree of value. The values, of course, differ. Some are more, and some are less, fundamental and primary. Of course, moreover, one might urge that there are other tests, equally fundamental. There is the test of the practice of hard work, there is the test of the use of leisure by the individual, there is the test, too, some would say, of the cardinal virtues. Such tests, I am sure, have worth, and perhaps they may be found inherently in these, no less than a dozen in number, which I have outlined.

And now I come to the pointed question, for the

asking of which preceding paragraphs have prepared the way. Does America, does the United States, meet these tests?

(1) The first test applied is this: Does the United States respect its past? The answer is an unequivocal yes. Of course there are parts of this vast country which do not respect its past. But, giving due weight to exceptional conditions and associations, the general answer does hold good. America respects the English settlement at Jamestown, the Pilgrim settlement at Plymouth, the Puritan settlement at Boston, and the Dutch settlement in New York. It respects the Revolution and its leaders, it respects the Civil War and its leaders, both Abraham Lincoln and Robert E. Lee. It respects the great movements, social, political, literary, religious, educational, which have made America.

(2) Furthermore. America is creating and maintaining institutions. Every century of her three hundred years and every Commonwealth of her vast area bear witness to the fact, and to the usefulness of these foundations. Some of them, like Harvard College, and William and Mary, were founded in the seventeenth century. More have their origin in the eighteenth, and a far greater number still in the nineteenth. Churches, library associations, banks, industrial and commercial agencies, literary unions, social combinations, abound. In fact, there is reason to say that the tendency to form institutions has become a

constructive force and a primary movement in the new American world.

(3) A similar answer is to be given to the third question: the movement toward the combining of human and other forces. For combinations are a condition out of which and into which institutions grow and which in turn result in further combinations of men and of things. The so-called trust represents the movement. The amalgamation of steel companies illustrates it. The union of great railroads confirms it. The system of chain stores combining thousands of individual units forms an outstanding and common example. The whole coöperative movement, of money, of work, of humane service, under diverse forms, is a timely and pregnant instance.

(4) To the first three tests America gives a clear and absolute response. But to the fourth the answer is obscure. Is the United States altruistic? The evidences are far from conclusive. A part of America is certainly selfward. It is concerned with itself. Its own prosperity seems to be its chief interest. My prosperity, my work, my success, my opinion, is to me controlling. Such an interpretation belongs pretty fully to certain classes. It belongs also somewhat to all classes. It is found in the so-called social zone, but not there alone. It is found in all zones which may be characterized as intolerant and which are concerned far more with their rights than with their duties. But there is a body of American citizens

to whom altruism is normal in intellectual interpretation, controlling in conscience and in will. It represents international patriotism as well as national. It is more concerned with duties than with rights. It is moved by specific ideals and is bathed in the atmosphere of idealism. As it is composed largely of those who may be called gentlemen, so likewise it believes in the Gentlestate as a political entity.

(5) A fifth test is waiting to be applied to America. It is the test of the future. Do the forces now created and acting promise to her a lasting greatness? The answer is even more obscure than that which obtains in the consideration of the fourth test. In point, however, of material and physical advancement, the answer is clear. For her natural resources are apparently inexhaustible. Coal, iron ore, and oil, these three dominant forces abound and apparently are to abound. Their exhaustion lies far ahead in the centuries. Leaving out unknown China and Brazil, no part of the world's territory has apparently resources so rich in these three forces as has the United States. The water power, too, is measureless. But when one turns to certain other forces, human largely, one becomes less certain. The lack of respect for law, for observing law's precepts, and for the assessment and enforcement of law's penalties, the love of physical pleasure, the difficulty of uniting peoples of diverse origins, of different racial strains, of opposing social ideals, beliefs and practices—

all these considerations give to the interpreter a distinct pause. Yet when one considers other elements such as the good feeling prevailing among all classes for each other, when one recognizes the lessening antagonism between capital and labor, when one reflects on the constant mobility of American life, there being no permanently servile class, when one recognizes the spirit of beneficence which moves the privileged portion of the community, the evidence becomes full of promise that America's sun is far from its setting.

(6) But interpretation becomes positively pessimistic when one is brought face to face with the condition of the American family. The American family, based like the family of every nation, on the exclusive love of one man and one woman for each other, has as an institution passed away. Its foundation in marriage has lost the popular respect which it formerly commanded. The conjugal relation is entered upon without proper forethought, the contracting parties knowing that it can be easily dissolved. A new name, "companionate marriage," awakens only a sense of dismay, for its meaning, standing for a duration of the conjugal union only so long as the contracting parties wish, is simply and only a recognition of the common conjugal practice. The obligations of the marriage bond are easily flung aside. Absolute divorce in certain States may be secured on trivial grounds, such as abandonment or non-support for a brief period, or even "incompatibil-

ity." Divorce, too, is often the result of collusion between the husband and the wife. The result is that in certain Commonwealths, or in certain counties of several Commonwealths, there is one divorce for every three marriages.[1] The future of the United States interpreted in terms of the fundamental institution of the family is indeed dark. This darkness is created or is recognized by conditions and causes as diverse as the "divorce mill" of the State of Nevada, or as the courts of France annulling the marriages of American citizens.

(7) Concerning a seventh test of civilization, it is easy to give a definite answer. For the United States is a unique example of the union of the stable and of the flexible in civil and political administration. The federal system of the United States is the most impressive illustration of its type of government wrought out by the mind and will of man. The very name gives a proper interpretation: It is a government of individual Commonwealths joined together in a great Union. It has in one hundred and fifty years proved its stability. It has also proved its quality of adjustment, both internal and foreign. The shock of civil war it has withstood. Over the disintegration caused by pernicious and obscure forces it has

[1] In the year 1924 in Ohio had one divorce for every 4.21 marriages, in Oregon one for every 2.36, and in Nebraska one for 2.23. In the United States as a whole, in thirty-seven years, the proportion has fallen from one divorce in 17.30 marriages to one divorce in 6.89 marriages.

triumphed. It has been firm without stubbornness, and yielding without collapsing. A government firm unto fixedness may fall in revolution or revolt. Think of recent histories. A government, like a ship, should have a spirit for yielding to the storm; but also should have a power for self-salvation. It should not yield too far. If it do, it ceases to be a government. The adjustment of the forty-eight individual States to each other, the adjustment of them each to the Federation, the adjustment of the Federation to the individual State, the committing of all international affairs to the Federation, these and all other diverse matters of local government and of the Federal, represent a stability and a flexibility which give promise of permanence.

(8) The respect paid in the United States to a further test, that touching the regard given to the community's life and health, presents interesting contrasts. The health of the people is protected by many rules, laws, and prohibitions. The boards of health of the city, of the country, of the individual States, and of the general government are efficient. Unofficial associations like the Red Cross are of commanding force and of consummate value. Both the official and the unofficial bodies act in epidemics and in such catastrophes as earthquake, flood and fire, with speed, power and efficiency. The general remedial forces as seen in the medical and nursing professions are of unexampled worth. The constant examinations given

to children in the public schools, for their health, examinations usually of much thoroughness, form an example of the care taken by the people for the health of the next generation. But the disregard for human life as seen in protecting it from accident, and catastrophe, is in dire contrast with the regard paid to it in the prevention and cure of disease. Absolute recklessness characterizes the American people in respect to the prevention of accidents. The record of the havoc wrought by the automobile, for instance, is a history like the history of an army in a retreating and fighting campaign. The casualties caused by the automobile in a period no longer than the period since the United States ceased fighting in the Great War are practically as great as were the deaths in that war of American soldiers. In respect to the regard to the preservation of life from violence the United States is not a civilized State.

(9) America meets, or fails to meet, the test of the sense of value touching property in a degree quite similar to that in which it meets the test touching the preservation of life from disease. The belief is common that America lives in and for and by the material and the materialistic. The belief, like most communal beliefs, is at once true and false. America does prize property, both real and personal, and real property, be it added, far less than do the English people. But the regard paid to property of both sorts is a regard rather for power than a regard for possession. To get

property the American labors long and hard, and to increase property he economizes, either ploddingly or fiercely, and ever constantly. But also the typical citizen, in his amassing property, takes tremendous risks, risks which, of course, go against him from time to time. But be it also emphatically said that America is distinguished quite as much by its gifts and bequests to education, to religion, and to charity, as by its struggle for the power which property represents. These gifts and bequests are taking on more and more the form of foundations or commissions: corporations to which are committed in trust vast sums for certain specified or general purposes. The Carnegie, the Rockefeller, the Commonwealth, Foundations or Boards are possessed of hundreds of milions of dollars. These trusts are administered with wisdom, discretion, faithfulness. They are an epitome, a microcosm, of the sense of value which the typical American attaches to property. For the typical American, if he regard property as an object to be gained, regards it also and more as a tool, an agency, a force, for usefulness.

(10) America is on the whole far less materialistic than is commonly believed. The idealistic interpretation is nobly illustrated in the respect paid to the mind and to the creations of the mind. Of course a discrimination is at once to be made. There is an America of the coarser and crasser sort which cares not for the idealistic and intellectual concerns; but the better America, the rul-

ing America, the prevailing America, has the broadest, deepest, highest appreciation of these noblest and most lasting values. The physician in his researches, the scientist and inventor in his discoveries, the lawyer in his interpretations, the college professor in his searchings for truth and in his declarations of truth, command the respect of the American people as do no other members of the community.

(11) The value of this test, which is the eleventh, as applied to mind in the American community, becomes still more significant when it is applied to education as a means of making mind. For if there be any one element in which America does believe, it is education. The evidence for the conclusion is seen in the single fact that about one-third of the whole American people is now actually, positively, engaged in the process of being educated. The evidence is also seen in the fact that, taken the country over, the best buildings for school, for college, for university, are gladly and gratefully built by taxpayer or by individual donor. Once the church was the foremost formative and constructive element in American society. One must now confess, and with the profoundest regret, that it is so no longer. Its place has been taken by the school and by the college. Of course the system of education has its weaknesses. Its primary weakness in its popular, or lower grades, lies in the brevity of the tenure, in the lack of richness and of culture of character, and

also in the want of full professional training, on the part of teachers. In its higher forms the weakness of American education is found in its very success, the over-population of its colleges. But taken all in all, education is the most important part of American life, and, as a test of that life, education gives a satisfactory interpretation of its civilization. The new and forceful movement, too, for the education of adults is a most timely illustration.

(12) The twelfth and last test which I apply is the test of religion. America cannot meet this test with the full responsiveness with which it meets the test of education. In the normal Protestant churches are found at least 42,000,000 members or adherents. The number of members or adherents in the Roman Catholic Church it is impossible to state accurately. The number is probably not far from 18,000,000. The remaining millions represent conditions, beliefs, and lack of beliefs, of all sorts and kinds. The unbeliefs, be it said, are far more common than anti beliefs. Skepticism is more normal than infidelity, and infidelity than atheism. The lack of the religious element in the beliefs of the American people is due to several causes: First, absorption in the present, in contrast with interest in the historic or the future relations of man; second, absorption in work in contrast with reflection; third, devotion to morals and ethics serving as a substitute for devotion to and belief in a Supreme Being; fourth, devotion

to pure philosophic idealism which serves to take the place of religious worship. The American, therefore, cannot be called a religious people in that fullness of meaning in which it is called a people devoted to education. Yet be it said it is a people which desires to be religious. It is seeking for a God. Its beliefs in heresies, or semi-heresies, in cults, in religious fads of many sorts are evidence and illustrations. Leaders and apostles of "faiths" rise with each rising sun, and, it may be added, also set with each declining day. America will, I believe, return to its early and better self, in accepting religion pure and undefiled. But at present it hardly meets this test of civilization.

As one reads over these applications, so numerous, so diverse, what result emerges? Does America meet the tests of civilization? It does fully meet the test of appreciating its past and of recognizing its future. It does meet the test of setting a proper value on the building of institutions and of forming coöperative combinations of citizens. It does, on the whole, meet the test of altruism, of the union of stability and flexibility in the civil government, of the appreciation of the value of life and of health (with a certain exception) and of respect for property. It does not at all meet the test of respect for the family or of respect for religion. As I put these tests into the judicial balances I find that the judgment inclines to the conclusion that America does meet these great tests of civilization.

XI

GROWTH OF INSTITUTIONS IN AMERICAN SOCIETY *

From the individual to the group, from the group to the movement, from the movement to the agency, from the agency to the institution, represent present social progress. The United States has passed, and is still passing, through such a trend. The last station in the fivefold hegira is now reached. The arrival, moreover, intimates an enlargement of the institutional conclusion. This enlargement, as found in several forms or fields of American society, deserves interpretation.

The first field which I seek to interpret is the Federal Government itself. For the Federal Government is of primary and fundamental importance. The instrument which represents the foundation of this Government, the constitution, has been, since its creation in 1787-8-9, the object of constant debate and of legislation. The debate and legislation have been concerned with the powers, rights, duties of the Federal Government in relation to the individual Commonwealth, and also with the rights, powers, and duties of the indi-

* April, 1930.

vidual Commonwealth in relation to the Federal Government. The trend of all the discussion and of all the laws has been to strengthen and to enlarge the functions of the Federation and to narrow and to weaken the function of the individual Commonwealth. This tendency, coming to its executive climax in the Civil War of 1861-65, has resulted in the comparative supremacy of the Government at Washington. The power of the Federal Government has constantly strengthened, and the power of the individual States has just as constantly narrowed. In his thought of his Government the individual citizen has come to think chiefly of the United States, and in his political loyalty has come to feel his pledge given not to his State but to the United States. The Stars and Stripes has come to be his flag, and the flag of his Commonwealth, even if it have one, commands no peculiar allegiance. In the year 1889, Bryce prophesied "the importance of the States will decline as the majesty and authority of the National Government increase."[1] The prophecy made forty years ago has with each succeeding year proved to be true.

The enlarged dominance of the Federal system becomes manifest in many forms and through a wide diversity of methods. Perhaps the most significant of all these forms and methods is seen in the creation of many so-called bureaus and commissions. These bureaus or commissions are in-

[1] *The American Commonwealth,* by James Bryce, Vol. II, p. 695.

dependent forces which the general government has established, and through which it functions. They are neither legislative nor executive, nor judicial alone, but are all functions combined. Their number and their manifold works are most impressive. The executive department of the Government in its divisions of the Cabinet has no less than 149 bureaus. The State Department has 20, the Treasury 17, the War 24, the Navy 19, the Post Office 21, Labor 8, Commerce 11, Agriculture 15, the Interior 9, and the Department of Justice 5. In addition there are some fifty commissions which represent a method and a force both legislative, executive, and judicial. These commissions are concerned with services as important and diverse as interstate commerce, shipping, the fine arts, the public lands, and lighthouses.

Without reference to the legislative or the judicial functions which, existing from the beginning, have enlarged their field and their forces, the executive department has come to possess and to use powers of control, to cultivate fields of influence, to enlarge functions, which represent one of the great institutions of history and one of the mighty forces of the modern world. It has, or it is, Authority. The Roman Empire covered and cultivated a wider area, but in a larger part of this area it failed to use so great a power as the United States uses in every part of its territory. The British Government today also covers a wider area, but in many parts of that area it declines to exercise the powers which the United States exercises in Commonwealths as remote from its center and from each other as are the Commonwealths of Washington and of Florida, of California and of the State of Maine. The growth in and toward a sense of institutionalism in the Federal Government is most significant and impressive. The growth is broad as well as fundamental, creative and formative of other institutions, and apparently ultimate in destiny. More and more completely does it become the *United* States.

In contrast with the general authority of the Federal Government there is a second institution, an institution which the Federal Government has so far consistently and firmly declined to direct, and that is the institution of education.[2] Education in the United States is a matter of the individual Commonwealth. It is the State which gives education to its children. The chief form of education is public, supported from the kindergarten through all the grades to the university, by public taxation. Of course, by the side of public education are found private schools, colleges and endowed universities. Education has become the consuming interest of the people, both in the public and in the specially chartered institutions. One-fourth of all the citizens of the United States are enrolled in her schools and colleges. No less than one million students are found in her col-

[2] A few minor exceptions exist, as is seen in Alaska.

leges and universities. In the last forty years the increase in college enrollment has been eightfold. The increase in the cost of all schools has in a half-century been no less than thirtyfold. The annual cost of public education is more than two billions of dollars. The so-called higher education takes on two special forms: the one of establishment and administration by the State, as is manifest in fifty universities; and the other of the privately chartered institution, like Harvard, Yale, Princeton, Columbia. The public universities are found in each of the great States, and in certain States no less than three, as in Ohio. Though the privately chartered institutions were of the earlier foundation, they have continued to grow with the growth of population and of resources. The growth, too, is commensurate with the growth of the State universities, like California, Illinois, Minnesota. At almost an even rate are the great universities of each type, maintaining themselves, whether supported by public taxation or by fees and individual gifts and bequests. The university of the State has hardly developed more swiftly than have the historic, privately chartered institutions. Harvard and Yale have in the last years each received annually sums running from eleven to twenty three million dollars. The State Universities have likewise spent commensurate sums in their annual administration. Their students, too, gathered from all parts of the world, represent an even more impressive evidence of institutional growth. New York University and Columbia enroll more than 30,000 students each in both internal and extra-mural classes.

The increasingly institutional character of the university is made yet more evident by the enlarging influence which it has gained on the manifold life of the whole community. All that concerns the community has come to concern the university. The many and diverse departments of the university serve communal needs diverse and fundamental. Its teachers' colleges train students to teach kindergarten, and also to pursue research as a professional quest. The University establishes and conducts schools as different as schools of business and of theology. The University, in fact, has become the crown of the broadest as well as of the highest intellectual life.

Carlyle's remark that a university is simply a great collection of books is a charming half-truth. Its half-truth represents a side of the institutional values of the university in American life. For the higher education in the United States is manifested in libraries having over forty millions of volumes. These academic collections, however, are only a part, about one-fourth, of the nearly ten thousand libraries now established. Taken altogether, the public and academic collections constitute an institution which is helping to form, to reform, to transform, American life. The number of volumes in the public libraries exceeds one hundred million copies. The annual expense for books and for administration is about forty million dollars. Cleveland has 1,000,000 people, and a free library of more than 1,000,000 volumes. These volumes are wisely selected. The support is derived from public taxation. The administration is committed to a thousand officers. The circulation represents eight volumes each year for each citizen. It has a central building, but also its usefulness is enlarged by more than a thousand branches or agencies. Libraries of this general type are found in every American city. They are graduated to the diverse and manifold needs of the community. In thousands of towns and villages libraries of a similar efficiency, adjusted to the size and demands of the population, are established. The American people are transmuting their American public library and the private collections into an institution. The American is usually described as primarily a reader of the newspaper. But he is also, and possibly more, a reader of books. That there are wide areas without such services is a fact, and a fact also to be deplored. The constant tendency, however, is to give the book to every child and to every adult.

The printing-press, of which the book is a fundamental product, does, however, manifest itself most conspicuously in the newspaper. This manifestation becomes more and more institutional with each passing decade. The institutional relation of the newspaper movement takes on at least two aspects. One aspect concerns the material part. The material part is indeed both expressive and impressive. Of course the number of such publications, twenty-five thousand, is evidence of the trend. The number of issues, too, some fifty millions a year, is evidence yet more convincing. The fact, too, of the transformation of the individual newspaper into a chain of papers is evidence both unique and conclusive. No less than fifty newspapers, divided almost equally between two groups, represent the essential part of this new development. The chains stretch from the Atlantic to the Pacific coast, and from the northern lakes to the southern gulf. Subject to a general control by a central agency, they yet are permitted a certain degree of liberty in the selection of news to be published, and in editorial interpretation. These selections and interpretations are, be it added, determined largely by local conditions. The power of such aggregations is simply colossal in forming and guiding public opinion. It has been said that it was a chain of American newspapers under one control which made the Spanish-American War. The Yellow press, or the Red press, forceful selfish factors, imposing itself on the Yellow or Red emotions of the American people, emotions which are not thoughts, has power to cause harm which transcends belief. It is a press, sober in feeling and sober in mind, appealing to the thinking citizen, which is called upon to put down irrational and swiftly-stirred emotions. Usually such an appeal overcomes the emotional explosions in case time be sufficient. But often time is not sufficient. The explosion bursts forth, creating a popular demand. The people are made to feel that they must fight, as they did fight upon the sinking of the *Maine*.

Beside such institutional organizations as are seen in chains of newspapers, there are found organizations known as the Associated Press or the United Press. These corporations are formed to collect and to disseminate the news of the world. Several such associations exist, but of them, two are chief. The larger, the Associated Press, has one thousand or more members. If there is a Yellow press or a Red press, the Associated Press might be called the White press. For its whole purpose and its comprehensive method are to convey all news in the white light of truthfulness as clearly and fully as the able and unprejudiced mind can conceive.

There is, however, at least one respect in which the newspaper press of the United States is failing. It concerns leadership. There is no journal which commands the allegiance and the following of the people. It is hardly too much to say that there is no journal of opinion. There are, as I have indicated, vast forces, powerful, fair-minded, for collecting the news of the whole world, forces lodged in individual papers like the *New York Times* and in various press associations. But there is no journal comparable as a journal of opinion to the *New York Tribune* of the years when Horace Greeley was its editor and dictator. The policy of trimming is now too common in many outstanding journals. In the United States is found no newspaper which commands the traditional place of the London *Times* as a journal of opinion, formative of public judgment. Possibly, too, journals of opinion in America are to pass over from the field of daily, into the field of weekly, issue. Such a trend is becoming evident.

As uniting both the governmental and certain popular elements of the tendency to establish institutions, the banks, the trust companies and other financial concerns present significant evidence. The new importance of the United States as a financial force is seen as both cause and result in the place which the banks have come to occupy in the whole life of the people. It is said that the United States holds about one-half of all the gold of the world. The larger share of this value is controlled by banks. A constantly enlarging share is coming to be held by a few banks in a few great cities. This fact, however, should be linked with another fact, that one-half of all the people in the country are depositors in either savings or other institutions. Such a concentration and also breadth of capital is new to the world. American banks are, moreover, taking on new forms. Among them is the form of what is known as chain banks—in which one organizing or supervising corporation maintains a certain advisory relation to many coördinated institutions. Another form is what is called branch banks, a system by which one central institution establishes several offices in one central city or at other capital points more or less widely scattered. This centralizing movement of capital is most manifest at its highest degree of power in what is known as the Federal Reserve system. This system had its origin at the time of the World War. The Federal Reserve system provided a means by which the enormous expenditures of the war could be met and the country's finances maintained on a stable basis. The expanding needs for currency were supplied by issuing Federal Reserve notes, partly secured by gold and partly by commercial paper. Banks were thus able to meet expanding needs for credit because they could supplement their reserves by borrowing from the Reserve banks or on customers' paper. The sum of money thus supplied was stupendous. It would have been sufficient to pay all the costs of the Federal Government from the year 1791 to the outbreak of the Great War. The previous expenditures for war were insignificant in comparison. The sum was equivalent to twenty times the national debt of the pre-war period.

Since the close of the war, the Federal Reserve system has been continued by wise methods and to results most beneficent. It has, as a fact, come to have a certain supervision over all the banking interests of the country, a supervision which at times seems to amount to control, even to effective control, and, I venture to add, to beneficent control.

Neither does such control or institutional consolidations relate alone to the present. They touch the long and indefinite future. For testators are more and more generally entrusting their estates to banks and trust companies. The individual administrator, executor, trustee, is being supplanted by the company or institution. The amount of property which is thus year by year, decade by decade, transferred to these fiduciary societies represents stupendous sums. At times it almost seems as if half of the property of the American people is becoming vested in these fiscal societies. In fact, it is said that no less than one hundred billions of dollars represent the actual or potential assets and responsibilities of life insurance companies.

The institutional life of the United States, both as a fiscal and as a personal form of endeavor, is furthermore manifested in the agencies which the community has set up for the cause of charity and philanthropy. Of course the words charity and philanthropy have a connotation as comprehensive as humanity, and as diverse as humanity's needs. But in the United States in recent decades and years the enlargement and the increasing variety is most significant. So-called foundations, as Community Fund, Community Chests, Community Trusts, have since the beginning of the Great War come to number more than sixty, and with the resources of thirty-two societies established before the year 1914, have come to possess resources of above a billion dollars.

These foundations represent the filling of the diverse needs which arise in a communal life of all sorts and conditions. They belong to forces as different as agencies for the establishing of international scholarships, societies for research into the causes of disease, and associations for the promotion of peace, for the elevation of the depressed races, and for the uplifting of the "unprivileged classes." The two thousand separate agencies for social betterment, established in New York City, and the more than one hundred agencies included in the Community Chest of a city like Cleveland, of a million people, prove the place and power of the philanthropic and institutional movement. The individual donations of the two great givers of the United States, Andrew Carnegie and John D. Rockefeller, illustrate the same trend. Mr. Carnegie endowed eight permanent foundations with no less than three hundred and fifty millions of dollars, and the known gifts of the Rockefellers, father and son, up to the present time aggregate six hundred millions. The larger share of this sum has been assigned to the endowment of five permanent foundations. Both the Carnegie and the Rockefeller gifts represent institutions. Their very names prove the strength of the institutional tendency. Among such names are the Carnegie Foundation for the Advancement of Teaching, the Carnegie Endowment of International Peace, and the (Rockefeller) General Education Board.

No small share of the charitable and philanthropic institutions of more recent foundation are devoted to medical research and to therapeutics. There is, however, yet another field of human service in which a still further form of the medical institution is coming to prevail. The profession of medicine, the most personal of all the professions, is taking on a special institutional relation. This relation is well summed up in the word Clinic. The clinic has long been recognized as an integral though subsidiary part of the hospital. It is now assuming a new form of human service. It is coming to mean a form in which several physicians are united for the examination and for the treatment of the sick. It stands for a union and for a sub-division of medical service. It is a transfer from a service in which the individual physician is the center to a service in which several physicians are combined for diagnosis, for the healing and for the prevention of disease. Several clinics are established in various parts of the country, of which two are the more outstanding, the Mayo Clinic in Rochester, Minnesota, and the Cleveland Clinic in the city of Cleveland, Ohio. This form of an institution is now already well founded, and be it said it is sure of coming to possess a great place in the healing forces and conditions of the American community.

The institutional trend of the United States is indicated, therefore, in these seven fields which I have sought, though briefly and summarily, to interpret: the Federal Government; the colleges and universities; the libraries; the newspapers; the financial institutions; the charitable and philanthropic institutions; and the medical foundations.

But there are two institutions which, it ought to be said, have not advanced in recent years. They are institutions central and constructive. They are the family and the Church. The family is both an historical and a social institution. It lies at the very heart of civilization both old and new. It is not strengthening. It is attacked by the general enemy of excessive individualism. It is menaced by many and swiftly changing social forces. It is threatened by the so-called enlargement of women's rights, which, however good in itself, may for the time being injure the home. Woman's enlarged rights have gone beyond the field of her duties. These disintegrating forces, many and different, come to their head in the increasing frequency and variety of divorces. Not far from one-fifth of the marriages in many commonwealths of the American Union end in divorce.

Likewise the Churches are not gaining in their institutional values and forces. I now write of the churches Protestant. With churches Roman

Catholic this paragraph and this article is not concerned. The enrollment of members increases, although slowly. But the recognition given to the Church does not increase in degrees adequate to the increase of population. The Church has lost largely its former educational function. It has also transferred its function of charity to specific agencies. It still retains, and apparently is to retain, its function of worship and of preaching. The clergy are devoted, both in pastoral administration and in preaching. But the response of the congregation is not adequate to the allegiance and the faithfulness in which the minister and the priest serve. To consider the causes of the narrowing conditions, or of a condition which certainly does not enlarge, would carry one too far afield. It is sufficient for the present purpose simply to intimate that the Church and the family are not growing as institutions to the degree in which other institutions like education and philanthropy are gaining. Be it said, moreover, that these two institutions are primary and fundamental.

However, a sufficient number of important institutions have been brought forward to prove the greater place and enlarged function which these foundations have gained for themselves in the United States. I therefore now turn to a problem more critical and constructive, namely, the causes and the conditions which have given birth to this tremendous result in the growth of institutions. Of the causes I wish to name three, and of the conditions two. Between these causes and these conditions, however, it is hard, and perhaps unnecessary, to discriminate. For causes flow into conditions, and the conditions easily become causes.

The causes of the growth seem to me to be summed up in efficiency and complexity. The will for efficiency is a strong will in the American character. "The will to will" is a possible change in William James's great phrase. The will to will eventuates, through the union of personalities, in the institution. Along with this will, moreover, goes a desire for the smallest possible expenditure. Efficiency, moreover, stands for mass production, for comprehensiveness. It is opposed to the individualistic method. It is contrasted with æsthetic values. It represents the quantitative in contrast with the qualitative. It spells amounts. It connotes creativeness. Such a will, such economic and economical methods, place emphasis on a central and centralizing government, on mass education, on huge financial agencies, on chains of newspapers, on aggregations of charities and philanthropies, on vast accumulation of books, and on a centralized medical service.

A second cause of the institutional growth lies in the increasing complexity of the community's life. Modern life has become complex, uniquely complex, disastrously or gloriously complex. Every morning ministers to or hinders the day's work of each citizen in the revelations of the doings of the globe. The telegraph, the telephone, the radio, deliver the world at every breakfast table. Such diverse and multitudinous offerings must be consolidated, classified, united. The individual cannot bear up against such offerings of individualized service, doings, and imaginations. The foundation of institutions is therefore the normal method and conclusion of procedure.

Such causes beget conditions for their creation and for their application from what I may call the mass: first, the mass of wealth; secondly, the mass of population. Wealth has become, as I have intimated, enormous in this new country. Such massing of wealth nourishes the enlargement of the general government and the foundation and increased power of the other institutions which I have considered. The massing of population, too, embodies and prepares the way for the foundation of institutions. Institutions like the higher education, or like the enormous banking consolidations, could not be founded or maintained in the thinly populated prairies of North America or on the more thinly populated pampas of South America. Such great populations do, indeed, represent individualisms and the whole individualistic movement of society. Such individualisms and such movements may create forces and make achievements of much worth. Of course, in the whole historic trend of society they have created such forces and such movements; but great wealth and great populations are also conditions necessary for forming great institutions.

A matter quite as essential as the question of the conditions and causes of this institutional movement, is the question of the results of this force upon American society and life. Is this movement to permeate and to characterize all American life and conditions? Is it to create groups of power, to influence, to gather up and to centralize the elements of these groups, and to project them into the whole American community? In this consolidation, is the individual to be submerged? Is the smaller to shrivel up into the less, and into the least? Is the much to grow into the more, and the more into the most? Is America to form a race of many sub-men and of a few super-men? Is humanity to become, like the modern office building, narrower as it goes higher? Is the common man to become a mere cog in a colossal and swiftly-turning machine? Is the movement to become mightier than the men who compose the movement? Are men, fabricating a Frankenstein, half conscious that the creature may prove to be a fiend which will ultimately turn on its fabricators and destroy them? Is force, material and executive, to become more and more forceful; and reflection just a shadow so far and so far only as may be necessary to guide this force, even if with dimness? Is the unhumanized system and the dehumanized group to rise or to fall into absolute monarchism?

Or is it to be recognized that these movements are above all else movements of, for, and by men? Is it appreciated that their origins, their progress, their failures, their consummations are human, humane, humanistic? Is it seen that the degrees of their merit, that the worth of their contributions, represent racial well-being and racial enrichment? Is it understood that the enlargement of the individual is a symbol and method of the enlargement of the race, and that the withering up of the individual is the minimizing and shrivelling of all humanity? Is it felt that the economizing in certain so-called lower forces and forms of life may give a freedom for the transmutation of these lower forms into terms of a loftier dynamics, dynamics which deserve the name of spiritual?

Such questions spring to the pen. In response to them I wish to say:

First: The present condition of American and of world society is one of experimentation—political, social, educational. Man, the experimenter, wishes for, and is determined to have, the best. No conclusion, therefore, is to be regarded as final and conclusive. Therefore, no lover of his kind need fear that the present consummation is to rest down on mankind with the weight of the mountains or to transfix mankind in the bonds of human iron and steel.

Secondly: Humanity is interested in terms of life, and not in terms of the lifeless. Its interest is to be interpreted in terms of development. It stands for growth. Behind and before both growth and development lies life.

Thirdly: The institutional movement represents association and adjustment. Each part of it ministers to every other part, and every part which receives ministers to every other. The civil government serves the educative, the philanthropic, the social, the financial, the domestic, and other forms of being. Each of these in turn serves the civil function, each aiding every other. Of what worth any one of these institutions without education? Of what worth any one of them without the stabilizing power of the civil government? Of what worth any one of them without the substratum of the financial? Each survives because the other survives.

Therefore, a comprehensive conclusion of this survey is fearlessness. American humanity is not to become a mere series of institutions unrelated, unassociated. Man is not to be made a *schema* of big, disconnected conglomerates. Man, putting his life into institutions, is thereby, if he be at all worthy, to find a life fuller, a character nobler, a comradeship more intimate, a usefulness broader and more continuous, a destiny which without loss of individuality becomes deeper and higher, and a prophetic sense of realization more divine.

INDEX

Acton's library, allusion to, 138
Adams, Henry, allusion to, 30-31
Altruism, test of civilization, 223ff
America, educational conditions, 26ff; in religion, 33ff; sufficiency of to herself, 188ff; remoteness of, 198; past of, 232; combinations in, 233; family in, 235ff; divorce in, 236ff; flexibility in government of, 236ff; health in, 237ff; property in, 238ff; less materialistic than believed, 239ff; education in, 240ff; religion in, 241ff; faiths, so-called, in, 242; institutions in, 232ff, 243ff; social fearlessness of, 263
American, community, 9ff; materialistic, 16ff; student, 28; literature, 30ff; newspapers, 32; Civil War and Great War, 92ff; church and the Great War, 165; people, unused strength of, 165-66; heart, tenderness of, 189ff; Protective Association, allusion to, 196; education, interpretation of, 211ff; civilization, 221ff; respect for tests of civilization, 232ff; altruism, 233; regard for future, 234ff
American Society, the best and worst in, 1ff; the American family, 40ff; the Pilgrim's motive and contribution, 58ff; the effect of the European war on higher learning in, 70ff; the American Civil War and the Great War: a comparison, 92ff; prospects of liberal education after the Great War, 121ff; public opinion in the United States in the three years: 1914-1917, 144ff; after the Great War, 160ff; ruling ideas in, 187ff; Shauvenistic, 187ff; what are the tests of a nation's civilization? 221ff; growth of institutions in, 243ff
Americanization, 167; and world history, 167, 168
Amusements, American, 18
Andover, allusion to, 35; Theological Seminary, allusion to, 192
Aristotle, reference to, 221
Arnold, Matthew, reference to, 128; quotation from, 169
Arnold, Thomas, allusion to, 199
Arts, fine, 18ff
Asquith, allusion to, 159
Authority, governmental, 245ff

Bacon, allusion to, 44
Bancroft, allusion to, 30-31
Banks, reference to, 252ff
Bay Colony versus Plymouth Colony in absence and presence of learned men, 61ff; other contrasts, 67
Beecher, Henry Ward, allusion to, 165
Bernhardi, allusion to, 77
Best and worst in American society, 1ff
Bible, lack of knowledge of, 38; reference to, 66; after the Great War, 174ff

Biology and the Great War, 72ff
Birthrate, among Harvard classes, 52; and family, 52ff; Wesleyan University, 53
Bismarck, reference to, 160
Bradford, William, reference to history by, 64; quotations from, 65, 66
British colonial policy and Great War, 81
Brooke, Brian, reference to, 131
Brooke, Rupert, reference to, 130
Brooks, Phillips, allusion to, 165
Bryce, Lord, judgment by, 30-31; American respect for, and for his works, 157-58; quotation from, 181-82; quotation from *American Commonwealth* of, 244
Business after the Great War, 178ff

Calvin, allusion to, 2
Cambridge, England, tutorial system of, 30; versus Oxford, 61
Capital and labor after the Great War, 179ff
Carlyle, allusion to, 248
Carnegie, Andrew, allusions to, 4ff, 218; reference to, 255ff
Carnegie Foundation for Advancement of Teaching, allusion to, 213
Cartesian philosophers, 44
Chain banks, reference to, 252ff
Channing, reference to, 206
Charity, interpretation of in America, 254ff
Choate, Joseph H., allusion to, 163
Christian Science, growth of, 208ff
Christ's College, Cambridge, allusion to, 59
Church, Protestant, divisions in, 36-37; American, and the Great War, 165; after the Great War, 171ff; Roman Catholic, reference to, 210ff; allusion to, 257ff
Civilization, American, 221ff; tests of, 221ff; tests of in America, 232ff
Clergy after the Great War, 176
Cleveland, City of, allusion to, 249
Clinic, in Cleveland, 256; medical, 256ff
Colleges, graduates of, callings of, 207ff
Combinations, test of civilization found in, 223
Commemoration Ode, Lowell's, 31
Commissions as form of government, 244ff
Community, American, 9ff; thoughtful group in, 17ff; chest in Cleveland and other cities, 255ff; complexity of, 259ff
Congress, federal, making laws, 13
Constitution of United States, allusions to, 3, 12ff
Coulson, Leslie, reference to, 131
Cowie, A. G., reference to, 131
Crile, George W., allusion to, 71

Dante, allusions to, 2, 14
Declaration of Independence, allusions to, 2ff, 45
DeTocqueville, quotations from, 14, 205 (quotations from, 14, 205)
Dewey, John, allusion to, 78
Dexter, F. B., allusion to writing of, 60 note
Dishonesty, evil of, 5-6
Divorce, reference to, 11; in America, 236ff
Doctrine, Monroe, allusion to, 190
Downing, the, professorships,

quotation from address of, 214 (Downing, the, professorship)

Ecclesiasticus, quotation from, 19-20
Economics and the Great War, 86ff
Education, in America, 26ff; vocational, 28ff; professional, 29; reference to, 46ff; and religion to be united, 69; liberal, prospects of after Great War, 120ff; liberal, definition of, 121ff; liberal versus education for efficiency, 123ff; liberal, more than intellectual, 123ff; German, primarily intellectual, 125; liberal, duty of emphasis on history, literature, philosophy, religion, 136ff; after the Great War, 180ff; American, interpretation of, 211ff; respect for, test of civilization, 230; in America, 240ff; interpretation of, 246ff
Edwards, Jonathan, allusion to, 64
Efficiency of individual, 7; in American character, 259ff
Elder Brewster, allusion to, 58-59
Emerson, allusion to, 31; reference to, 206
Emotionalism in religion, 37
Epicureanism, 41ff
Eucken, allusion to, 78
European war and American society, 70ff
Executive, action, ruling idea in America, 200ff; in government, 203ff
Experimentation in America, 262

Faiths, so-called, in America, 242
Family, place of, 10ff; versus individualism, 10ff; neglect of religious training in, 38; American, 40ff; legal sanctions of, 50ff; restoration of, 50ff, 57ff; and birthrate, 52ff; and the Roman Catholic church, 54ff; religious sanctions and the, 54; after the Great War, 170ff; respect for, test of civilization, 225ff; in America, 235ff; allusion to, 257

Federal, system of government, 21ff; laws of immigration, 192ff; government, taxation by, 217ff; government, interpretation of, 243ff
Federal Reserve system, reference to, 253ff
Fichte, reference to, 76
Flexibility, in nation, test of civilization, 226ff; in government of America, 236ff
Foreign missions, 35
Foundations, Rockefeller, Commonwealth, 15
Freedom, after the Great War, 185-86; religious reference to, 207
French Revolution, 45
Freston, H. Rex, reference to, 130
Future of a nation, respect for, test of civilization, 225

Gentlestate, the, and Great War, 90; allusion to, 224
German, student, 28; language and literature in schools, 156
Germany, and World War, 71; public opinion in United States regarding, 154ff
God, mind of, respect for, test of civilization, 230ff
Goethe, allusion to, 139
Government, federal system of, 21ff; American, new questions concerning, 25; civil, after the Great War, 177ff
Graham, allusion to, 131

Grant, U. S., allusion to, 116-17
Great Britain, Spain, contrasts in, 224ff
Great War, and effect on subjects of study, 72ff; biology and the, 72ff; modern languages and the, 73ff; research studies and the, 75ff, 85; philosophy and the, 76; and religion 78ff; and social sciences, 79ff; and international law, 81ff; and British colonial policy, 81; and economics, 86ff; and history, 88ff; and the gentlestate, 90; and American Civil War, 92ff; the American church and, 165; family after the, 170ff; individualism after the, 170ff; church after the, 171ff; mysticism after the, 174; Bible after the, 174ff; Sabbath after the, 175ff; clergy after the, 176; civil government after the, 177ff; business after the, 178ff; capital and labor after the, 179ff; education after the, 180ff; professional education after the, 182ff; woman's education after the, 183; freedom after the, 185-86
Greeley, Horace, letters to, from Lincoln, 95, 115
Grenfell, Julian, reference to, 130
Grey, Sir Edward, 158-59

Haeckel, allusion to, 78
Happiness in family, 40ff
Harvard college, allusions to, 27, 29, 53, 59; reference to, 206
Hay, John, allusion to, 163
Health, respect for, test of civilization, 227ff; in America, 237ff
Heart, American, tenderness of, 189ff

History and the Great War, 88ff
Hodgson, W. N., reference to, 131
House of Commons, 32

Idealism versus sordidness, allusion to, 4
Indiana, State of, allusion to, 42
Individual person, best in society, 2ff
Individualism, versus family, 10ff; and modern life, 47ff; after the Great War, 170ff
Institutions, test of civilization, 222ff; in American society, 243ff; reference to, 255ff; causes and conditions of growth of, 259ff; result of, 261ff; human relations of, 262ff; representing association and adjustment, 263
Intellectual class in America, 191ff
International law and Great War, 81ff

James, William, allusion to, 78

Kaiser, the, allusions to, 80, 161, 162
Kant, reference to, 76; allusion to, 139
Kitchener, allusion to, 166
Know-nothing movement, allusion to, 196
Ku Klux Klan, reference to, 195ff

Labor and capital after the Great War, 179ff
Lea, Henry C., allusion to, 30-31
Lee, Robert E., allusion to, 117
Leisure, place of, 19-20
Legal sanctions of family, 50ff
Legislators, character of, 201ff
Leipzig, allusion to, 192
Lessing, allusion to, 139
Leyden, Pilgrims at, 62ff

INDEX

Liberal education, prospects of after Great War, 120ff; definition of, 121ff; duty of emphasis on history, literature, philosophy, religion, 136ff
Liberty, in United States, 2ff; and patriotism in American Civil War and Great War, 98ff
Libraries in America, 248
Lincoln, Abraham, allusion to, 68; quotations from, 93ff; 100ff
Literature, American, 30ff; American versus English, 31-32; spoken versus written, 32-33
Lloyd George, allusion to, 159
Locke and sensational philosophy, 45
Long parliament, allusion to, 68
Longfellow, allusion to, 31
Lowell, J. R., allusions to, 31, 163

Maine, H. S., quotation from, 39
Materialism in America, 16ff
Mayo clinic, 256
Medical quackeries, 15
Mildmay, Sir Walter, reference to, 61
Mill, John Stuart, quotation from, 56-57
Milton, reference to, 45
Mind of man, respect for, test of civilization, 229ff
Modern languages and the Great War, 73ff
Modern life and individualism, 47ff
Modern world new physical world, 126ff
Monitor, Christian Science, reference to, 209
Monroe Doctrine, allusion to, 190
Morley, Lord, quotation from, 138
Motley, allusion to, 30-31

Mysticism after the Great War, 174

Newspapers, American, 32; types of, 249ff
New York City, allusion to, 5

Oxford, tutorial system of, 30; versus Cambridge, 61; allusion to, 192

Page, W. H., reference to, 188
Palmer, George Herbert, quotation from, 79 note
Parkman, allusion to, 30-31
Past, the respect for, 221ff
Pasteur, allusion to, 14
Peirce, Benjamin, quotation from, 26
Perry's victory on Lake Erie, reference to, 162
Peter House college, Cambridge, 58-59
Philosophy and the Great War, 76
Pilgrim, foundation, 34ff; motive and contribution, 58ff
Plymouth Colony, increase in population of, 59; public schools in, 59; versus Bay Colony in absence and presence of learned men, 61ff; other contrasts, 67
Pope Leo XIII, quotation from, 55
Population, massing of, 260ff
Prescott, allusion to, 30-31
Princeton, allusion to, 29
Pritchett, H. S., quotation from, 213ff
Privileged classes, the, reference to, 215ff
Professional education, 29; after the Great War, 182ff
Professorships, exchange, 135-36
Property, respect for, test of civilization, 228ff; in America, 238ff
Protestant, church, divisions in,

36-37; reformation and family, 43ff; religion primary, 209ff
Protests in American Society, 197-98
Psalm CXXXIX, quotation from, 121
Public opinion in United States 1914-1917, 144ff; surprise, inquiry, irritation, horror, antagonism, 147ff; democratic movement, 151ff; socialism, 153ff; regarding Germany, 154ff
Puritan foundation, 34ff, 44

Radcliffe, A. V., reference to, 131
Ratcliffe, S. K., references to, 195ff, 200
Red Cross, reference to, 15
Reformation, Protestant and family, 43ff
Religion, in America, 33ff; emotionalism in, 37; primary to the Pilgrims, 63; and education to be united, 69; and Great War, 78ff; power of, 140ff; as fundamental in war crisis, 164-65; as ruling idea, 205ff; Protestant, primary, 209ff; in America, 241ff
Religious, sanctions and the family, 54; freedom, reference to, 207
Research, 26ff; studies and the Great War, 75ff, 85; medical, 256ff
Restoration of family, 50ff, 57ff
Revolution, French, 45
Rhodes, scholarships, allusion to, 135
Robinson, John, quotation from, 62; farewell letter of, 63-64
Rockefeller, John D., allusions to, 4ff, 218-19; reference to, 255ff

Roman Catholic church, and the family, 54ff; reference to, 210ff
Rousseau, allusion to, 45
Royce, allusion to, 79 note

Sabbath after the Great War, 175ff
Sanctions, legal, of the family, 50ff; domestic, of the family, 51ff; religious and the family, 54
Schiller, allusion to, 139
Scholarship, books of, 18
Schopenhauer, quotation from, 76 note
Sciences, social, and Great War, 79ff
Seeger, Alan, reference to, 130-31
Separatists, 62
Socialism, allusion to, 9-10; reference to, 153ff
Socrates, allusion to, 143
Smith, Ralph, 59
Society, American, the best and worst in, 1ff; the American family, 40ff; the Pilgrims' motive and contribution, 58ff; the effect of the European war on higher learning in, 70ff; the American Civil War and the Great War: a comparison, 92ff; prospects of liberal education after the Great War, 121ff; public opinion in the United States in the three years: 1914-1917, 144ff; after the Great War, 169ff; ruling ideas in, 187ff; Shauvenistic, 187ff; what are the tests of a nation's civilization? 221ff; growth of institutions in, 243ff
Sorbonne, allusion to, 192
Sordidness versus idealism, allusion to, 4
Sorley, C. H., allusion to, 130; quotation from, 139

INDEX

Spain, Great Britain, contrasts in, 224ff
Spencer, Herbert, quotations from, 7-8
Spinoza, allusion to, 64
Sports, 18
Sterling, Robert, reference to, 130
Stewart, Viscount Andrew John, reference to, 130
Stieglitz, Julius, quotation from, 131-32
Sufficiency of America to herself, 188ff; Superficiality in America, 28ff

Taxation, representing both the best and the worst, 23ff; formal and informal, 23ff
Teacher, worth of, 142ff
Teaching, weakness in, 29-30
Teapot Dome case, reference to, 6
Times, London, allusion to, 252; New York, allusion to, 251

Treitschke, allusion to, 77
Tribune, New York, allusion to, 252
Tufts College, quotation from address of president of, 133-34

Vocational education, 28ff

War, European and American society, 70ff; and medical schools, 71ff
Washington, George, allusion to, 68; reference to farewell address of, 215
Wealth, massing of, 260ff
Webster, Daniel, quotation from, 6
Williams College, allusion to, 192
Williamstown, allusion to, 35
Woman, independence of, 48ff; education of after the Great War, 183

Yale college, allusion to, 27, 29